SEEiNG WiTH NEW EYES

A GUiDEBOOK ON TEACHiNG & ASSESSiNG BEGiNNiNG WRiTERS

Assessment and Evaluation Program
Northwest Regional Educational Laboratory
101 SW Main Street, Suite 500
Portland, Oregon 97204

ACKNOWLEDGMENTS

The Northwest Regional Educational Laboratory would like to express its sincere appreciation to the students, teachers and staff who have contributed to the publication of this 5th edition of *Seeing with New Eyes.*

Ms. Billie Rice and Fran Hunter: writing and portfolio ideas
Arlene Moore: teaching inspiration
Lenore Hay: samples of student writing
Nancy Caslick: linking writing and art
Jollee Ellis: scoring criteria for primary students
Sara Knight: writing portfolio
Zaneta Revels: artistic contributions
Northwest Regional Educational Laboratory staff:
endless contributions to turn an idea into reality

This book is lovingly dedicated to Mrs. Arlene Moore, one of the finest primary teachers ever to grace a classroom, and to the students of the 1995-96 Lincoln Elementary transitional class, Mt. Vernon, Washington, who taught us so much about being better teachers, writers, and researchers.

Seeing with New Eyes

Table of Contents

INTRODUCTION

Welcome! If you are a primary teacher, you already know how special the world of the young writer is. At this level, "writing" may take the form of pictures, scribbles, dictated stories and thoughts, recordings, or conventional text. Sometimes that text goes left to right on the page, sometimes right to left, or bottom to top, or round in spirals. Primary writers are imaginative, and their writing often reflects a mixture of creative, highly individual style, and an attempt to adhere to the conventions of print—as interpreted through primary eyes.

This collection of student writing and drawing and teacher ideas attempts to place all these differences in perspective, and to view the experimentations and playfulness of students not as errors, but as ways of learning. Our text is respectfully dedicated to the writers of today and tomorrow and the wonderfully patient and insightful teachers who are forever looking for ways to encourage them. We hope it helps you find appropriate and inspiring ways of responding to your young writers' work.

Assessment & Evaluation Program

Northwest Regional Educational Laboratory

Der Gog.
   Can.I kOm.hows.
 and tac you
 prSnt.

        LoVe,
        Tasha

Dear George,
    Can I come to your house and
    take you a present?
        Love,
        Tasha

Tasha's letter

as seen through traditional eyes ...

What do traditional forms of assessment tell us about Tasha's writing? Well, her spelling is inaccurate, for one thing. The punctuation is arbitrary—and confusing. Words are omitted. The whole thing is difficult to read. It's short. It doesn't say a lot. Such assessment reflects a host of traditional expectations about what writing is or should be. But do those traditional expectations give us a true picture of Tasha's writing skill? Not really ....

Tasha's letter

as seen through new eyes ...

Suppose we put content, voice, and purpose before conventions, and view early conventions developmentally, asking, What is Tasha noticing in the print that fills her world? What is she borrowing?

Now, through "new eyes," we see that Tasha is recognizing the power of print. She knows you can get attention through what you write, and that one appropriate form of communicating is with a letter. Her letter follows traditional format, with an opening or salutation, a body, and a closing. She also uses left to right orientation on the page, plus up to down orientation, which makes her writing easy to follow. She has spaces between her words. A few words are omitted, true enough, but we can easily infer what they are.

The spelling may not be conventionally correct, but Tasha captures so many of the sounds of her language that the text is really quite readable; that's real developmental progress for a first-grade writer. She starts names with capital letters. Notice that the comma in the closing is used correctly;

Tasha has indeed been paying attention to how letters begin and end. The periods are tossed about at random, yes, but this writer knows periods are important—and that in itself is a beginning.

Her voice is emerging, and will gain strength from practice and from her awareness that her writing can have power and influence. Her message is direct, purposeful, and very understandable. Short, yes. But length will come with experience and confidence. On the pages that follow, we offer more ideas for seeing young writers' work <u>through new eyes</u>.

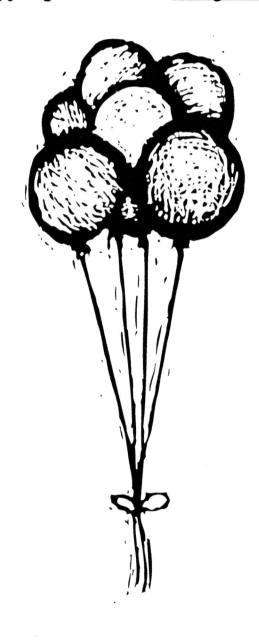

Chapter 1

"Seeing" the Traits

One day a kindergarten teacher said, "I'm not sure these traits are relevant to my students' work. Fluency? Why does it matter? My students don't even write sentences."

Not with paper and pencil perhaps. Not <u>yet</u>. But they hear sentences. And speak them. That is where it all begins.

To really see how the six-trait model fits primary students' work, we have to take an expanded (and probably more accurate) perspective on writing. We have to stop staring myopically at desktops and move back just a little, making the world of writing bigger. Let the world of writing take in the bookshelves along that wall, the colored posters over there, the conversation in the corner, the view out the window. Writing is thinking, feeling, reading, listening, responding, playing with language in our heads, talking to friends, planning, loving the sound of words, hearing the beat of language much as we hear the beat of a song on the radio. Have you ever watched primary students listen to music and move with the rhythm? Clap hands, move and stamp their feet, whirl, dance? That is the beginning of fluency. To hear the beat.

Loving to hear it might lead, <u>could</u> lead, if we nurtured it, to a love of poetry and rhythmic, graceful prose. Wanting to be read to, then to read aloud to others might lead, <u>could</u> lead, if we encouraged it, to a sense of what a sentence is, then a playfulness with word strings that turn into sentences. And if we read aloud enough, often enough, from works that were good enough, it might lead, probably <u>would</u> lead to a skillful crafting of sentences that were clear, logical, insightful, and lyrical. Iambic pentameter couplets? Who can say?

HOW IT BEGINS

We must ask of each trait, how does it begin? How does it look at first?

Ideas don't show up first as detailed, complex prose or irrefutable statements bulwarked by lusty statistics. They begin as astute observations that show an attentive mind: the rough sketch of a beetle with six legs and layered wings (the artist had to look closely to notice those things).

Organization doesn't begin with the Stephen King-style lead that won't allow us to put a book down even at 2 a.m., or the elaborate, skillful sorting of multiple data bits, but as balanced placement of art, scribbles, or text on the page, coordination of art with text, or use of a title to indicate the official beginning.

Voice is not, at first, the subtle self-deprecating humor that fills Garrison Keillor's tales of the Midwest or the sarcasm of Dave Barry or the eloquence of Maya Angelou. Not at first. It's a picture that speaks to you through its color or energy, a word, a turn, a twist, a subtle surprise that makes you smile, a style of writing or sketching or thinking or speaking that is individual and spirited, or a connection to the writer that makes you say, "Oh, that's so like Sara."

Word choice is not in its early stages the haunting echoes of Carl Sagan's reverent tribute to the cosmos. It begins as a whimsical, playful curiosity about words that are first spoken, heard, noticed, remembered—and eventually (if spoken and heard enough) written down.

Conventions do not begin with precise spelling, strategically placed semicolons, knowledgeable manipulation of gerunds and participles, or impeccable grammatical style. They begin with creative borrowing. Noticing that prose moves from left to right on the page (most of the time), that people read from top to bottom (most of the time), that so-called sentences end with tiny dots and begin with letters that are bigger and (often) shaped differently, that letters (associated with sounds) sometimes stick up and sometimes hang down, and come in <u>thousands</u> of forms (How many fonts are there? How many different handwritings?).

If you ever worry whether students will learn conventions, ask yourself how much they have noticed and learned and borrowed already. If we, as adults, continued to notice and borrow at this same breathtaking rate, we would be writing everything from business letters to poems to government proposals and technical manuals with an editorial finesse and precision that would dazzle even the talented and knowledgeable authors of the <u>Chicago Manual of Style</u>.

---

*I*nventive spellers' errors don't interfere with their learning to spell correctly later. Like early attempts to walk, talk and draw, initial attempts to spell do not produce habits to be overcome. No one worries when a child's first drawing of a person is a head propped up on two stick legs. As the errors become more sophisticated—two stick arms protruding from the head where the ears should be—no one fears this schema will become a habit, though it may be repeated a hundred times.

Susan Sowers

"Six Questions Teachers Ask About Invented Spelling"

Understanding Writing, 62

TAKING ADVANTAGE

How do we take advantage of students' borrowing powers, curiosity, listening skills, and energy? How do we teach traits of writing to young writers, long before they are writing sentences and paragraphs, long before some are even writing words or letters?

We remind ourselves that students can hear and picture ideas, hear and think about organization, recognize and respond to voice, love the sound of words, and both hear and feel fluency long, long before they can create these things in their own written text. So, we teach through reading, sharing the best literature we can find.

> Children exposed only to basals may indeed learn to read, but they find the stories so lifeless and so tedious that they wonder why people *bother* to read: they don't become lifelong readers because no one has ever given them a reason to be lifelong readers. We need real books in the classroom, books beautifully written and beautifully produced, wild books, funny books, scary books, sad books, loving books, short books, long books, picture books, chapter books, nonfiction books—anything that will create *rewarded* readers.
>
> *Mem Fox*
>
> *Radical Reflections*, 64

We also remind ourselves that for many students, pictures are a natural and comfortable form of expression. Within students' art, we see evidence of detailed thinking and observation, individual voice, and the balance that is an early form of organization. If we learn to look for these things, we can point them out to students.

We find many ways to share the language of writers, helping students to feel comfortable and at home with terms like "voice" and "organization" and "conventions."

We can put the pencils down now and then, and allow students to do the same, encouraging them to dictate some pieces, or to tell stories orally. Then we will hear their true sense of fluency, the vocabulary that lives in their heads but that, for many, far surpasses what their fingers can create.

We can also write ourselves, thereby creating for our students something most of us never had: a model of a writer at work. Through writing, we learn to solve writers' problems:

- Where do I get ideas?

- If I wrote on something once, can I write on it again?

- Should I express this idea in words or pictures?

- If I use pictures, do I need more than one?

- What do I do if I can't spell a word?

- What other word will fit here?

- What's a good title for this?

- How do I know when it's finished?

- How long should it be?

- How big should I write?

- Who will read this?

If we only ask our student writers to solve these problems, and we never solve them ourselves or talk about how we solved them, we are only assigning writing, not teaching it.

Teachers write in class not to impress children with their superior skills, but to show that even adults often have better ideas the second time around … . If Dr. Seuss writes one thousand pages to produce a sixty-page book, then surely it's all right if a rank beginner in the first grade has to scratch something out.

Donald Graves and Virginia Stuart

Write from the Start, 87

YOU ARE INVITED ...

to look within the following pages for many more ideas on teaching young writers to think like writers by using the language of the traits. You will find ...

- **A host of TEACHING IDEAS linked to the traits**
- **Thoughts on using PORTFOLIOS (and a sample of one student's portfolio)**
- **Suggestions for using ORAL READING to teach the traits (if you love reading aloud to students, you're already doing one of the most important things you could do to build writing skills)**
- **Tips on teaching beginning writers to be EDITORS**

... and much more. So, let's begin.

Chapter 2

HOW THE TRAITS SHOW THEMSELVES AT PRIMARY LEVEL

Strengths in the traits show up right from the earliest writings. We just have to know what to look for. They do look a little different in the work of young writers! But we can train our eyes to see the beginnings of writing skill.

For instance, suppose a child scribbles intense, dark lines in all directions on the page. We may not be able to read it in the traditional sense, but we can still find a way to connect it to the traits: "Just look at all the feeling you put into this picture! Your work has a lot of voice."

Or, we might say, "Look at the detail in your picture of a spider! Eight legs and multiple eyes, too. Nikki, I think you have spent some time really looking at spiders."

On the pages that follow, we provide

1. **SOME DEFINITIONS**
   A definition of each trait, and a summary of how it looks at primary level.

2. **SIGNS OF THE TRAITS**
   A summary of what, specifically, to look for relative to each trait, and suggestions on the kinds of things you could say to reinforce strong performance—or <u>tiny</u> signs of success.

3. **THE SIX TRAITS—PRIMARY VERSION**
   An overhead master which provides a quick traits-at-a-glance summary of how these qualities of writing look at primary level.

SOME DEFINITIONS

IDEAS

Ideas are the heart of the message, the content of the piece, and the main theme, together with all the details that enrich and develop that theme. When the ideas are strong, the message is clear or the storyline is easy to follow. Things make sense. The secret all lies in the details: Strong writing always includes details that are clear, interesting, and less than obvious. Successful writers do not spend time telling readers what they already know: *Penguins are black and white, penguins live in Antarctica, penguins love to eat fish.* They seek out the details a reader might <u>not</u> know: *Penguins swim well because they are shaped like torpedoes. Penguins are territorial, and like some space around themselves and their nests. They will launch themselves at anyone who comes too close.*

HOW THIS LOOKS
AT PRIMARY LEVEL

At primary level, we need to look for details in children's artwork, and listen for important details in the stories they tell long before they begin to create extended text. Encourage students first to be gatherers and collectors of information, as well as observers of life, to look carefully at the world around them, and to share what they see orally, through their pictures and through their text. Later, as they write more, look for focus, meaning, a clear message or story, strong details, and direct statements like, "I like horses." When you see these things, help children see the power of their own writing, too!

Look also for complexity: lots of lines, lots of colors in pictures. Or, little important details that would have been easy to gloss over: veins in leaves, birds or insects with wings and legs, expressions on faces, details like buttons on clothing or shoelaces, signs of movement (a person running or waving, a bird poised for flight), words woven into pictures, perspective (small to large), or pictures that extend off the page.

ORGANIZATION

Organization is the internal structure of writing—like the framework of a building or the skeleton of an animal. It holds things together, and gives the whole piece form and shape. Good organization helps a reader understand a writer's message or follow a story with ease. A writer with strong organization stays focused on one key idea (in informational writing) or one main plot (in a story). The writer also fills the text (and sometimes the pictures!) with little clues that tie ideas together, and builds bridges (transitions) from one idea or event to the next. When the organization is strong, the beginning builds a sense of anticipation in the reader; the ending wraps things up in a satisfying way.

HOW THIS LOOKS AT PRIMARY LEVEL

At primary level, think balance and harmony. Early signs of organization include filling the page with text or pictures in a balanced way (the writer literally "organizes" text, picture, and white space), and creating labels, titles, or other text that harmonize with a picture. Gradually, primary writers also develop a sense of sequencing, which may begin with chronological order (for storytelling), then grouping (putting like bits together in informational writing). This kind of beginning structure may show up in picture sequences (two or more pictures) first, then in multiple-sentence text. Primary writers may also develop a strong sense of beginning and ending from listening to text long before they are able to reproduce these features in their own writing.

VOICE

The voice is the writer coming through the writing. It is the heart and soul of the writing, the magic, the wit, the feeling, the life, and breath. It is unique to each writer. When a writer is (1) engaged personally with the topic, and (2) aware of communicating with an audience, he/she imparts a personal flavor to the piece that is unmistakably his or hers alone. It is that individual something—different from the mark of all other writers—that we call voice.

HOW THIS LOOKS
AT PRIMARY LEVEL

Individuality! Sparkle! Love of writing, drawing, life itself. Exuberance. Humor. Playfulness. Emotion on the faces of characters. The extraordinary. These are the signs of voice. At primary level, voice is first noticeable in speaking, oral storytelling, and art. It is individual expression, independence, liveliness. In art, it may show up as a kind of energy in the work. It may reveal itself through facial expressions or pictures that create tension or a sense of anticipation in the viewer. Writers/artists with strong voice find their own paths, through pictures and later, through text. Their work tends to look different or sound different from that of others. It gets our attention. And it often makes us say, "Oh, I know whose picture writing <u>that</u> is." The something that tells you is voice.

WORD CHOICE

Word choice is the use of rich, colorful, precise language that communicates not just in a functional way, but in a way that moves and enlightens the reader. In good descriptive writing, strong word choice paints pictures in the reader's mind. In informational writing, strong word choice clarifies, explains, or expands ideas. In persuasive writing, strong word choice compels the reader to see things more clearly or, sometimes, to agree with the writer. Effective word choice is characterized not so much by an exceptional vocabulary as by the ability to use everyday language naturally and in a fresh or unexpected way.

HOW THIS LOOKS AT PRIMARY LEVEL

Primary writers/artists may express strong word choice in their oral storytelling or other sharing long before they write many words at all. Early on, we can listen for original expression, and note their curiosity about word meanings or usage. As they begin to write words, look first for the understanding that letters form words, and that written words communicate a specific meaning. Later, look both for correct word use and for originality, including a willingness to experiment—to try new words recently heard, or even to invent words! Look also for images, pictures, and ideas that evoke particular words or phrases: "When I look at this picture, the word that comes into my mind is power ... [or???]"

In text? Verbs, verbs, verbs. Words that show action, energy, movement. Verbs are important because they give the reader more information per word than any other part of speech. But unusual or precise or well-used nouns and adjectives and adverbs are important, too. Look for the unexpected, the writer who is stretching. One third-grader wrote, "My dog's ears were flourishing with thick fur."

SENTENCE FLUENCY

Sentence fluency is the rhythm and flow of the language, the sound of word patterns, the way in which the writing plays to the ear, not just the eye. How does it sound when read aloud? That's the test. Fluent writing has cadence, power, rhythm and movement. It is free of awkward word patterns that slow a reader down, and cause the reader to stumble or reread. Sentences vary in both length and style, and are so well crafted that reading aloud is a pleasure.

HOW THIS LOOKS AT PRIMARY LEVEL

Most primary writers are not writing sentences at the <u>beginning</u> of their primary years (a few are!). So of course, we cannot always look at sentence lengths or patterns, not at first. We will look at these things as soon as they show themselves. Till then, listen for rhythm and cadence in oral language, and notice how the writer attends, as a listener, to rhythm in the language you share orally. Is the listener in tune with sentence patterns, rhythmic language (such as poetry), or rhymes? Can your listeners/writers tell a sentence from a fragment or phrase? Can they tell rhythmic language from language that is choppy? What they hear they will begin to write. They will learn fluency as listeners first, then gradually reflect what they hear in the beat of their own text.

Once the sentences begin to flow, look <u>beyond</u> punctuation. Listen for the rhythm. Listen to one second-grader's paper on poetry ...

What is poetry?
poetry is moosick to me
on a pees of paper
moosick that rimes,
soft moosick to my ers

Also look at sentence beginnings. When you see differences, let the writer know you noticed. Does one sentence begin in a way that hooks it to the preceding sentence, e.g., *At the same time ... Then ... Next ... But ... When that happened ... Later ... The next day?* These links are important. They show logic. Are some sentences longer? You can point this out. But mostly—mostly—hear the sound. Hear the beat. Read aloud. Enjoy the flow.

CONVENTIONS

Conventions are textual traditions. They have grown out of a need for some conformity to make text penetrable and easier to follow. Anything a professional proofreader would deal with in getting text ready for publication falls under this heading: spelling, punctuation, grammar and usage, paragraphing, and capitalization. Neatness, while important, is not considered part of the six-trait model.

HOW THIS LOOKS AT PRIMARY LEVEL

Primary students are natural borrowers, and their knowledge of conventions shows up first in their borrowing. Keep in mind that even the simplest of things, such as writing from left to right, or beginning at the top of the page and working your way downward, or facing your E's the same way all the time, or putting spaces between your words must all, ALL be learned. No writer is born knowing these things. All are conventions of our accepted writing style. Notice and acknowledge these beginning conventions to give your primary writers a legitimate sense of their true accomplishment.

Discovery of periods or quotation marks (or any mark of punctuation) is cause for celebration—regardless of whether those marks are correctly placed yet. Exploration is a vital stepping-stone on the path to correctness. The writer who discovers periods will (soon) also discover how and when to use them. Similarly, students must first associate sounds (consonant sounds, then vowels) with letters and play with letter strings to form words before moving to prephonetic, phonetic, and close-to-correct or sometimes correct spelling. Readable spelling is a fine goal at primary level. Conventionally correct spelling is a lifelong goal which virtually no one (including professional editors) masters totally without the support of helpful resources (dictionaries and spell checkers).

Look then for creative and persistent borrowing. Reward your students for noticing the print around them (and provide plenty of it), and for being curious enough to ask questions. Encourage guessing about what a group of letters might spell, what a mark of punctuation might mean. This is the time of exploration, and exploration in itself is a major and significant conventional goal for the primary years—and for as long as we want writers to keep learning. (If you doubt its importance, visit a high school or freshman English classroom and ask how many students have <u>recently</u> read a style handbook or dictionary for fun, added a new convention to their editing repertoire, or showed enough curiosity about a mark of punctuation to ask how or why it was invented.)

On the following pages, you will find a brief trait-by-trait summary of what to look (or listen) for at primary level, and a short list of possible things you could say to a student to reinforce strengths in each of the traits. Remember that what you see first will not look like finished, polished, conventional writing. It may be in picture form, or scribbles we cannot decipher yet. It may or may not include any text whatsoever! That's **OK.**

In one child's scribbles and in another's portrait of a hungry dinosaur, you will see energy and (perhaps) a sense of excitement or passion. That's voice. In yet another student's sketch of an owl, you will see feathers carefully drawn to lie in different directions. There you have attention to detail: ideas. One student may be experimenting with

periods.and . placing .them .after .just about .every word .

She is borrowing from the world of conventions, and inviting you to notice her important discovery. Accept her invitation.

SIGNS OF THE TRAITS:
WHAT TO LOOK (& LISTEN) FOR
WHAT YOU COULD SAY

IDEAS
WHAT TO LOOK (& LISTEN) FOR ...

- Complexity (lines, colors)
- Attention to detail
- Noticing little things others might not notice
- Clarity, focus, sense of purpose
- A message or story, complete or not

To reinforce IDEAS,

YOU COULD SAY ...

- I know just what you mean!
- You're really using writing to communicate.
- I can really picture what you're telling me!
- No one else thought to write about Venus fly traps [or whatever]—how did you come up with such an original idea?
- I loved your topic/idea!! It made me think of ....
- You really notice things—look at these details!!
- What is the most important thing this author had to tell us?
- What do you picture in your mind when you listen to this writing?

16

ORGANIZATION
WHAT TO LOOK (& LISTEN) FOR ...

- Pictures and/or text balanced on the page
- Coordination between text and picture (they go together)
- Multiple pictures that show sequence
- Grouping of details, ideas
- Text that shows sequence: *First ... then ... after ... next ... later ... last ...*
- Text that shows connections: *Because ... so ... when ... however ...*
- Sense of beginning: *One day ... Last week ... When I was little ...*
- Sense of ending: *So finally ... That's all ... At last ... The end*
- Cause and effect structure in text (or picture series)
- Problem-solving structure in text (or picture series)
- Chronological structure in text (or picture series)
- Surprises that work
- Sticking with one main topic or idea

To reinforce **ORGANIZATION**,

YOU COULD SAY ...

- I can see how these ideas/pictures go together.
- You knew just how to begin (or end).
- This happened because this happened—that's a good way to organize ideas.
- You organized your story by time ... <u>first</u> this, <u>then</u> this ....
- I wanted to know what would happen next!
- What a surprise ending!
- You solved a problem—that's a good way to organize ideas.
- [When reading aloud] This story has the title _____ . What do you suppose it's about?
- So far this author has told us _____ . What do you predict will happen next? How do you predict this will end?
- Let me read just the beginning of this writer's story/essay. Is this a good way for the writer to begin? Why?
- Can you tell me back this story/essay in a few sentences?

VOICE
WHAT TO LOOK (& LISTEN) FOR ...

- Individuality
- Sparkle
- Personality
- Liveliness, playfulness
- Emotion
- The unusual
- Taking a chance by trying something new or different
- Recognizing that the writing/drawing is for both self and audience
- Tailoring communication to an audience
- Response to **VOICE** in the writing/art of others

To reinforce **VOICE**,

YOU COULD SAY ...

- Your feelings come through loud & clear here.
- I could tell this was you!
- This story/picture made me laugh/cry/feel what you must have felt.
- You seem to be writing to/for [*specify your best guess on audience*]. Is that right?
- I love the way you help your reader see & feel the things you are seeing or feeling when you write. There's a word for that—**VOICE**.
- Your writing rings with voice. It made me want to keep reading!
- Do you think the story we just read had **VOICE**?
- Which of these two pieces [share two samples orally] has more **VOICE** in your opinion? Why do you think that?
- If **VOICE** were a color, what would it be? If it were a food ... If it were a sound ... If it were a place ... .

18

WORD CHOICE
WHAT TO LOOK (& LISTEN) FOR ...

- Playing with letter forms, letters, letter strings, first words, labels, etc.
- Stretching to use new words
- Curiosity about words
- Verbs, verbs, verbs (energy words)
- Precise words
- Unusual use of words or phrases (in speaking or writing or labeling)
- Striking words or phrases
- Imitation of words or phrases heard in literature (or any reading you share in class)

To reinforce WORD CHOICE,

YOU COULD SAY ...

- I see you're making a connection between letters & words.
- This word/phrase goes well with this picture.
- I love this word—how did you think of it?
- What was your favorite word in the story we just read?
- What do you think the word _____ means? Make a guess.
- When you said <u>streaked</u>, I could really picture the whole thing ... .
- I love this word—<u>flourishing</u>—how did you think of it?
- This picture makes me think of the word [... ???].
- _____ was just the right word to describe/explain _____ .

SENTENCE FLUENCY
WHAT TO LOOK FOR ...
- Experimenting with word strings to form sentences
- Rudimentary sentences—subject & verb
- Use of more complex sentences
- Multiple sentences with different beginnings, varied lengths
- Rhythm, cadence in oral or written language
- Long & short sentences
- Love of rhythmic language (e.g., poetry)

To reinforce **SENTENCE FLUENCY**,

YOU COULD SAY ...
- I read this aloud & I love the sound of it!
- You seem to know what a sentence is—good for you!
- You have a long sentence, then a short one—I like that.
- Your sentences begin in different ways—that's great.
- I like this phrase—<u>After a while</u>—it helps me understand when things happened.
- Listen to this piece [read a fluent piece aloud]. Now, listen to this one [read the same one chopped into 3- or 4-word sentences that all begin the same way]. Do you hear a difference? Which one do you like?
- Here's one of my favorite pieces [choose one to read aloud]. I think it has rhythm. See if you hear it, too.

CONVENTIONS
WHAT TO LOOK FOR

- Left to right orientation on the page
- Up to down orientation on the page
- Letters facing appropriate directions
- Distinction between upper- & lowercase letters
- Spaces between words
- Spaces between lines
- Name on the page
- Use of a title
- Use of labels
- Use of indentation to show a new paragraph
- Dots over i's
- Exploration with punctuation, whether conventionally placed or not
- Rudimentary spelling, showing a connection of sounds to words
- Readable spelling (can be interpreted without the writer's help)

To reinforce CONVENTIONS,

YOU COULD SAY ...

- You remembered to write your name at the top—thanks!
- I love it when you put a title on your paper—it gives me a good clue about your message/story!
- You remembered to put spaces between your words—boy, that helps!
- I could sound out most of these words. I read it without any help.
- How did you know to put a comma/period/question mark/capital here?
- I notice you start on this side (left) & write this way (right); you're really paying attention to how books are written.
- I see you've discovered ellipses [or whatever is new]. Great! When you see that mark, what does it mean to you?
- When you work to make your spelling readable, it really helps your reader a lot. Super!

THE SIX TRAITS PRIMARY VERSION

IDEAS

- What is the message?
- Does it make a point? Does it tell a story?
- Details, details, details!

ORGANIZATION

- Beginning & ending
- Like things go together
- Balance on the page
- Order makes sense

VOICE

- Personality!
- Pizzazz!
- Flavor, charm, liveliness
- Individuality
- New, different, full of adventurous spirit

WORD CHOICE

- Using words correctly
- Trying something new
- Verbs!
- Flair, personal phrasing

FLUENCY

- Sentences hang together
- Sentence "sense"
- Variety
- Rhythm & flow
- An ear for language patterns

CONVENTIONS

- Left to right orientation
- Up to down orientation
- Letters facing the right direction
- Spaces between words—& between lines!
- Distinguishing between lowercase & CAPITALS
- Playing with punctuation (correctly placed or not)
- Knowing names of some conventions
- Copying environmental print
- Having readable spelling as a goal

Chapter 3

DeVeLOPMeNTAL CONTiNUUMS

GUIDES TO UNDERSTANDING

After a brief introduction, you will find four approaches to helping both teachers and students chart growth and accomplishment as writers. These are, in order of presentation:

Guide 1

6-Trait Assessment for Beginning Writers

Guide 2

Writing Criteria Trait by Trait

Guide 3

Holistic 6-Trait Assessment for Beginning Writers

Guide 4

Primary Writers' Very Own Scoring Guide

HOW TO USE THE GUIDES

You might clip one of the following sets of criteria into a child's folder or portfolio, so that you can use it as a checklist and celebrate together any new writing skills. At a parent conference, you might use the continuum checklist to help parents recognize writing skills and behaviors they may not have noticed in their young writers' work. You might use the criteria to formally document beginning writer growth over one, two or three years' time.

SHOULD I EXPECT A STUDENT WRITER TO BE AT ONE GENERAL LEVEL OF PROFICIENCY?

We have no such expectation. In other words, a given writer may be at the exploring level with regard to some skills and behaviors, but at the emerging or developing level with regard to others. In addition, some traits may emerge as strengths ahead of others; perhaps voice will precede organization for some writers, for instance.

The idea of drawing-as-rehearsal is just one more example of the word-centered view that reigns in our educational system. The child's drawing is reduced to a preliminary, a kind of pre-writing, rather than being accepted as an important communicative symbol system in its own right.

Thomas Newkirk
More Than Stories, 37

SHOULD I LOOK AT BOTH PICTURES & TEXT?

Absolutely. These primary guides are designed to reflect performance in both forms of communication, and recognize picture writing as a legitimate form of expression, not simply a transitional phase to writing with words. It is important for beginning writers, who often feel comfortable with picture writing, to see that their pictures do indeed contain detail, do express voice, and do reflect awareness of organizational balance, which may be as simple as filling the white space in a pleasing way.

WHAT IF A GIVEN WRITER IS AT THE FLUENT/EXPERIENCED LEVEL ON ALL TRAITS?

A writer who consistently (not just on one or two occasions, but routinely) achieves at the fluent/experienced level across all six traits, and who is writing text of two paragraphs or more in length, is probably ready (or right on the verge of being ready) for assessment on the regular six-trait assessment scales.

You can easily check this out by assessing one or two pieces of the student's work using the traditional six-trait scoring guide. See NWREL's web site www.nwrel.org/sixtrait for a copy. If the writer is ready, you will find this higher level scoring guide:

- **Easy to use**
- **Truly reflective of the writing qualities you see in the student's work**
- **More accurate & appropriate in describing the student's strengths than a primary level continuum**

A writer who is truly ready for assessment at that higher level should receive scores of at least 2 on most traits. If that does not happen, the student writer is probably still within the range of performance described in the primary guide. Continue using the primary guide for a while, then try the higher—level six-trait guide again once the student is writing longer and more complex text.

Within our classes there will be kids who can't tie their shoes and kids who can build electrical motors, kids who can't tell time and kids who can do double-digit division in their heads. These contrasts will be particularly dramatic in our reading and writing workshops. Many second graders can just barely read their names; others are devouring the entire works of Roald Dahl and Patricia MacLachlan. Some write only captions underneath drawings; others write long chapter books and research reports. Some children write with big, wobbly letters; others write with tiny, neat rows of cursive.

Lucy McCormick Calkins

The Art Of Teaching Writing, New Edition, 109

SIX-TRAIT ASSESSMENT FOR BEGINNING WRITERS

1 — EXPERIMENTING

IDEAS
- Uses scribbles for writing
- Dictates labels or a story
- Shapes that look like letters
- Line forms that imitate text
- Write letters randomly

ORGANIZATION
- Attempts to write left to right
- Attempts to write top/down
- No sense of beginning and end yet
- Experiments with spacing

VOICE
- Communicates feelings with color, shape, line in drawing
- Work is similar to everyone else's
- Ambiguous response to task
- Awareness of audience not present

2 — EMERGING

IDEAS
- Some recognizable words present
- Labels pictures
- Uses drawings that show detail
- Pictures are supported by some words

ORGANIZATION
- Consistently writes left to right
- Consistently uses top/down
- Experiments with beginnings
- Begins to group like words/pictures

VOICE
- Hints of voice present in words and phrases
- Looks different from most others
- Energy/mood is present
- Treatment of topic predictable
- Audience is fuzzy—could be anybody, anywhere

3 — DEVELOPING

IDEAS
- Attempts a story or to make a point
- Illustration supports the writing
- Meaning of the general idea
- Some ideas clear but some are still fuzzy

ORGANIZATION
- A title is present
- Limited transitions present
- Beginning but no ending except "The End"
- Attempts at sequencing

VOICE
- Expresses some predictable feelings
- Moments of individual sparkle, but then hides
- Repetition of familiar ideas reduces energy
- Awareness that the writing will be read by someone else
- Reader has limited connection to writer

4 — CAPABLE

IDEAS
- Writing tells a story or makes a point
- Illustration (if present) enhances the writing
- Idea is generally on topic
- Details are present but not developed (lists)

ORGANIZATION
- An appropriate title is present
- Attempts transitions from sentence to sentence
- Beginning works well and attempts an ending
- Logical sequencing
- Key ideas begin to surface

VOICE
- Writing is individual and expressive
- Individual perspective becomes evident
- Personal treatment of a standard topic
- Writes to convey a story or idea to the reader
- Attempts non-standard point of view

5 — EXPERIENCED

IDEAS
- Presents a fresh/original idea
- Topic is narrowed and focused
- Develops one clear, main idea
- Uses interesting, important details for suport
- Writer understands topic well

ORGANIZATION
- An original title is present
- Transitions connect main ideas
- The opening attracts
- An effective ending is tried
- Easy to follow
- Important ideas stand out

VOICE
- Uses text to elicit a variety of emotions
- Takes some risks to say more than what is expected
- Point of view is evident
- Writes with a clear sense of audience
- Cares deeply about the topic

Assessment and Evaluation Program. Northwest Regional Educational Laboratory, Portland, Oregon. 503/275-9500.

1
EXPERIMENTING

WORD CHOICE
— Writes letters in strings
— Imitates word patterns
— Pictures stand for words and phrases
— Copies environmental print

SENTENCE FLUENCY
— Mimics letters and words across the page
— Words stand alone
— Patterns for sentences not in evidence
— Sentence sense not yet present

CONVENTIONS
— Writes letter strings (pre-phonetic: dmRxzz)
— Attempts to create standard letters
— Writes word strings
— Attempts spacing of words, letters, symbols or pictures
— Student interpretation needed to understand text/pictures

2
EMERGING

WORD CHOICE
— Recognizable words
— Environmental words used correctly
— Attempts at phrases
— Functional language

SENTENCE FLUENCY
— Strings words together into phrases
— Attempts simple sentences
— Short, repetitive sentence patterns
— Dialogue present but not understandable

CONVENTIONS
— Attempts semi-phonetic spelling (MTR, UM, KD, etc.)
— Uses mixed upper and lower case letters
— Spelling of high frequency words still spotty
— Uses spaces between letters and words
— Uses capitals at the beginning of sentences
— Usually uses end punctuation correctly (.!?)
— Experiments with other punctuation
— Long paper may be written as one paragraph
— Attempts standard grammar

3
DEVELOPING

WORD CHOICE
— General or ordinary words
— Attempts new words but they don't always fit
— Settles for the word or phrase that "will do"
— Big words used only to impress readers
— Relies on slang, clichés, or repetition

SENTENCE FLUENCY
— Uses simple sentences
— Sentences tend to begin the same
— Experiments with other sentence patterns
— Reader may have to reread to follow the meaning
— Dialogue present but needs interpretation

CONVENTIONS
— Uses phonetic spelling (MOSTR, HUMN, KLOSD, etc.) on personal words
— Spelling of high frequency words usually correct
— Uses capitals at the beginning of sentences
— Usually uses end punctuation correctly (.!?)
— Experiments with other punctuation
— Long paper may be written as one paragraph
— Attempts standard grammar

4
CAPABLE

WORD CHOICE
— Uses favorite words correctly
— Experiments with new and different words with some success
— Tries to choose words for specificity
— Attempts to use descriptive words to create images

SENTENCE FLUENCY
— Simple and compound sentences present and effective
— Attempts complex sentences
— Not all sentences begin the same
— Sections of writing have rhythm and flow

CONVENTIONS
— Transitional spelling on less frequent words (MONSTUR, HUMUN, CLOSSED, etc.)
— Spelling of high frequency words usually correct
— Capitals at the beginning of sentences and variable use on proper nouns
— End punctuation is correct
— (.!?) and other punctuation is attempted (such as commas)
— Paragraphing variable but present
— Noun/pronoun agreement, verb tenses, subject/verb agreement

5
EXPERIENCED

WORD CHOICE
— Everyday words used well
— Precise, accurate, fresh, original words
— Creates vivid images in a natural way
— Avoids repetition, clichés or vague language
— Attempts at figurative language

SENTENCE FLUENCY
— Consistently uses sentence variety
— Sentence structure is correct and creative
— Variety of sentence beginnings
— Natural rhythm, cadence and flow
— Sentences have texture which clarify the important idea

CONVENTIONS
— High frequency words are spelled correctly and very close on other words
— Capitals used for obvious proper nouns as well as sentence beginnings
— Basic punctuation is used correctly and/or creativity
— Indents consistently to show paragraphs
— Shows control over standard grammar

Assessment and Evaluation Program. Northwest Regional Educational Laboratory, Portland, Oregon. 503/275-9500.

30

WRITING CRITERIA TRAIT BY TRAIT: IDEAS

The Exploring Writer

_____ Uses pictures to express ideas.

_____ Uses scribbles to express ideas.

_____ Creates shapes that imitate print or cursive text.

_____ Dictates story, message, or label for picture.

_____ Writes random "letters."

_____ Reader needs help to interpret pictures or "text."

The Emerging Writer

_____ Creates pictures and text reader can interpret with inferences and good guesses.

_____ Combines pictures with imitative text, letters, or "*just* readable" words.

_____ Uses labels to expand meaning.

_____ Pictures carry more meaning than text.

The Developing Writer

_____ Creates easily recognizable pictures and text.

_____ Creates stand-alone text that expresses a clear message.

_____ Attends to detail in pictures and/or text (more than a quick scribble or sketch).

_____ Text carries as much meaning as pictures—or slightly more.

The Fluent/Experienced Writer

_____ Creates pictures and/or stand-alone text that makes a point or tells a simple story.

_____ Elaborates on message or story.

_____ Incorporates the kinds of significant, less-than-obvious details that give both text and pictures interest, depth, and meaning.

_____ Presents ideas that catch a reader's attention.

_____ Shows knowledge of topic.

_____ Text carries most or all of the meaning (though pictures *may* be used to enhance meaning).

Assessment and Evaluation Program. Northwest Regional Educational Laboratory, Portland, Oregon. 503/275-9500.

WRITING CRITERIA FOR ORGANIZATION

The Exploring Writer

—— Places letters, shapes, scribbles, or pictures randomly on the page.

—— May fill one corner of the page or the whole page.

The Emerging Writer

—— Shows a growing sense of balance in placement of scribbles, text, or pictures.

—— Shows clear sense of coordination between text and pictures: e.g., a reader can readily see that they go together.

—— Begins to "center" work on the page.

The Developing Writer

—— Shows a beginning sense of sequencing or patterning (e.g., chronological order, main point and support) in written text.

—— Shows skill with story boarding (creating pictures in sequence to make a point or tell a story).

—— Writes multiple sentences in an order that supports a main point or story.

—— Shows a sense of beginning: *This is a story of... One day... My favorite food...*

—— Uses conventions such as title, indentation, numbers (1, 2 or first, second), and "The End" to help structure written text.

—— Presents work in a visually balanced way on the page.

The Fluent/Experienced Writer

—— Uses definite beginning and concluding statements (other than simply "The End") in text.

—— Uses transitional words and phrases (*next, then, so, but, while, after that, because,* etc.) to connect ideas.

—— Shows skill in sequencing a simple story chronologically. In informational writing, shows skill in

  • grouping "like" bits of information together

  • sticking with one *main topic*

  • moving from one support point to another (from where sea turtles live to what sea turtles eat)

—— Skillfully uses conventions such as title, indentation, or statement of purpose to structure text.

—— Creates a "complete" text. Doesn't just stop at the end of the page.

—— Presents work in a visually appealing way on the page.

Assessment and Evaluation Program. Northwest Regional Educational Laboratory, Portland, Oregon. 503/275-9500.

32

WRITING CRITERIA FOR VOICE

The Exploring Writer

____ May express feelings through use of vivid or varied colors, BIG "letters" or letter shapes, or bold, strong lines in picture text or scribbling.

____ Reveals voice through dictation.

The Emerging Writer

____ Creates pictures/text that express personality, feelings, moods, or individuality.

____ Creates pictures that seem to show energy, sense of motion, sense of anticipation, or events about to happen; characters with expressive faces or body language that projects strong feelings.

____ Uses exclamation points, underlining, BIG letters, bold lines, repetition (*very, very*), or other conventional devices to show strong feelings.

The Developing Writer

____ Creates pictures/text that show distinctive personal style, originality.

____ Expresses enough personality and/or feelings in pictures/text so that work can be linked to *this* writer by someone who knows him/her well.

____ Shows beginning sense of audience.

____ Creates pictures and text that produce an emotional response in the reader.

____ Uses conventional devices (e.g., exclamation point, capitals) to reinforce feelings, but voice comes through even without them.

The Fluent/Experienced Writer

____ Creates pictures and text that are expressive, individualistic, engaging, and lively.

____ Often projects a personal, individual attitude or point of view in work; it is clearly the writer's own.

____ Shows strong awareness of audience, and uses voice to influence the reader's response.

____ Creates writing that "speaks" to a reader in a definite and immediate way.

____ Projects a voice that can be characterized: humorous, whimsical, serious, intense, sad, angry, moody, sensitive, thoughtful, etc.

____ Occasionally uses conventional devices to underscore voice, but doesn't rely on them.

Assessment and Evaluation Program. Northwest Regional Educational Laboratory, Portland, Oregon. 503/275-9500.

WRITING CRITERIA FOR WORD CHOICE

The Exploring Writer

____ Copies words or letter shapes from environmental print.

____ Creates shapes or scribbles that represent words, even though a reader cannot yet translate them without help.

____ Writes in letter strings (all "letters" may not be recognizable).

The Emerging Writer

____ Writes recognizable words.

____ Uses labeling to enhance or "dress up" pictures.

____ Chooses words or labels or short phrases that clearly go with picture text.

____ Uses various parts of speech: e.g., naming words (nouns), describing words (adjectives), and action words (verbs).

The Developing Writer

____ Enjoys combining pictures with more extended text.

____ Uses expressive or descriptive phrases and short sentences, not just one- or two-word labels.

____ "Stretches" to use new words, even if she/he cannot spell them yet: e.g., *The lage harabel ants are planing to get the jucsy red appel from the bird.*

____ Creates text that conveys a clear general meaning: e.g., *My dog runs fast.*

The Fluent/Experienced Writer

____ Chooses words that make meaning clear and also create a particular mood or build a picture in the reader's mind: e.g., *Dad and the ball collided.*

____ Uses individual phrasing that enhances personal voice, e.g., *My dog's ears were flourishing with thick fur.*

____ Experiments with language in a variety of ways: imitating, inventing new words, rhyming, and/or looking for a particular "just right" word.

____ Relies only minimally on general words (*nice, great, fun, wonderful, special*).

____ Uses a variety of words, with little redundancy.

Assessment and Evaluation Program. Northwest Regional Educational Laboratory, Portland, Oregon. 503/275-9500.

WRITING CRITERIA FOR SENTENCE FLUENCY

The Exploring Writer

___ May use scribbles or imitative letter strings: LI EKPTLSSI NKT.

___ Does not yet write in sentences or word strings.

The Emerging Writer

___ Writes in word strings or simple sentence patterns (some sentences may not be complete).

___ Writes one sentence or an "almost" sentence: e.g.,
I LIKTOPLAY WITH MY BLOKS.
ME BIK AN THE SUN.

___ May use repetitive sentence patterns: e.g., I am a ball. I like be a ball. I lik Jim.

The Developing Writer

___ Writes in sentences; often includes more than one sentence in given text.

___ May imitate sentence patterns he/she has heard.

___ Begins sentences in different ways.

___ Creates text that another person can readily read aloud: e.g., I have a toy. The toy I have is my favrit toy and this toy is my bear.

The Fluent/Experienced Writer

___ Written text begins to imitate oral fluency.

___ Shows variety in sentence lengths and beginnings.

___ Writes as many sentences as he/she needs to complete the text.

___ Creates text that is easy for another to read aloud with expression.

___ Experiments with sentence fluency through some of the following:

  ___ varied beginnings
  ___ longer sentences
  ___ more complex sentences
  ___ use of dialogue
  ___ poetry
  ___ rhythmic patterns

___ Creates text with a natural, "easy flow" kind of sound: e.g., My name is watcher because I am an eye tooth. Just today I was cleaned. It sort of hurts but I've gotten to like it.

Assessment and Evaluation Program. Northwest Regional Educational Laboratory, Portland, Oregon. 503/275-9500.

WRITING CRITERIA FOR CONVENTIONS

The Exploring Writer

—— Experiments with print by

—— creating scribbles to represent text

—— creating scribbles that represent individual letters

—— May write with letter strings, usually pre-phonetic: e.g., SAMSAAUATT.

—— Can put own name (or a version thereof) on paper.

—— May create some recognizable letters or numbers: e.g., NATO2.

The Emerging Writer

—— Imitates many features of environmental print:

—— shapes that resemble letters

—— letters or letter shapes that face the right direction

—— left-to-right orientation on the page, up-to-down orientation on the page

—— blending of text with illustrations

—— Distinguishes between upper and lower case letters; begins to associate capitals with "important" words (may not always place capitals correctly).

—— Experiments with punctuation, especially periods, which may be randomly placed: e.g., I Luv. My Dog.

—— Writes own name on personal work.

—— Uses beginning (pre-phonetic) spelling with a *few* sounds—mostly consonants, few vowels: e.g.,
I lik t d nts
(I like to draw knights).

—— Continues to write with letter strings and short word strings, expanding to multiple words and simple sentences: e.g., I rn fast.

—— Often uses labels, titles, or both.

The Developing Writer

—— Incorporates more conventions from environmental print into own text:

—— spacing between words

—— spacing between lines

—— appropriate directional placement of letters—E, not 3

—— consistent left-right and up-down orientation

—— use of a title

—— margins

—— Uses both upper and lower case letters, (some of which may be randomly placed); often capitalizes "I," own name, names of others, and words of significance: e.g., I luv my Dog.

—— Experiments with other forms of punctuation: question marks, ellipses, commas, quotation marks, etc.

—— Expands to basic phonetic spelling with more consonant sounds and more vowels: e.g., I lik tu dru nts (I like to draw knights).

—— Writes own name and other significant words. Guesses at many words.

—— Uses inventive spelling well enough to create readable text: e.g., My dinosaur can bak. He ets fish. He is my frnd.

—— Usually places periods at the ends of sentences: e.g., I luv my dog.

The Fluent/Experienced Writer

—— Consistently incorporates conventions of spacing and directional placement of letters into own text.

—— Regularly uses both upper and lower case letters, and usually places them correctly: e.g., caps on names, caps at beginnings of sentences, capitalizing pronoun "I." May also capitalize words which are simply important to him/her: e.g., My Dog is my Frend.

—— Usually places periods and question marks correctly.

—— Continues to experiment with other punctuation: dashes, commas, colons, semicolons, ellipses, quotation marks, parentheses, and such. Places punctuation correctly, or makes a good guess.

—— Uses readable spelling for most words. Conventionally correct spelling of simple, familiar words: e.g., I like to draw knights (I like to draw knights). Good guesses on difficult words: e.g., The bright yellow sun reflects off the trueds (tremendous) airplane.

—— Writes more than one paragraph if needed.

—— Uses title if needed.

—— Uses margins.

Assessment and Evaluation Program. Northwest Regional Educational Laboratory, Portland, Oregon. 503/275-9500.

36

HOLISTIC SIX-TRAIT ASSESSMENT FOR BEGINNING WRITERS

This is a holistic look at writing growth, which charts five stages of growth and change:

- **Stage 1: Readiness**
- **Stage 2: Drawing & Exploring**
- **Stage 3: Confident Experimentation**
- **Stage 4: Moving Toward Independence**
- **Stage 5: Expanding & Adding Detail**

This five-stage overview does not attempt to capture all the nuances of accomplishment and behavior that mark primary writers' growth. It is an awareness overview that may help teachers, parents, and students themselves to see the role that experimentation, borrowing, and imitation play in everything from idea development to confident use of writing conventions.

> ### My Cat brock his Leg.
>
> In 1990 My cat brock his Legg beCuase he felled Off the roof It hAppen wen my bruthr lefed the dor opend And my dog rUnd out And saw my cat and chase him uP on the roof. And mY MOM got my Dog and put him in the House. I went. Up tO get Him. Put he tried to juMp dOwn and brock hiS leg on the drive wAy. We quik rushed Him to the vet. The vet. Said put a caSt on his leg and Went home. aNd my Cat went to sleP. The neXt morning. he was OK.

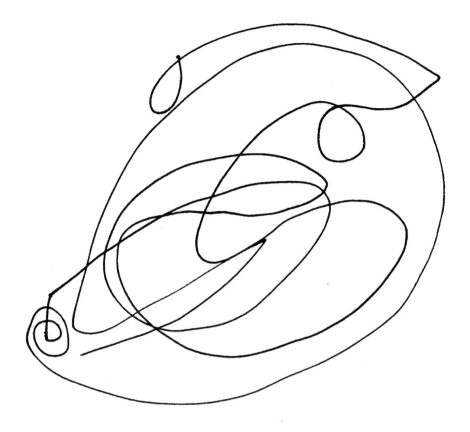

Stage 1: Readiness

The student

♥ Scribbles
♥ Notices print in the environment
♥ Shows interest in writing tools
♥ Likes to make marks on paper
♥ Begins to recognize the power of print
♥ Likes listening to stories, poems, etc.
♥ Begins connecting writing/pictures with self-expression
♥ Likes expressing himself/herself orally

Stage 2:
Drawing & Exploring

The student

- ♥ Draws pictures with recognizable shapes
- ♥ Captures more feeling in art through motion, color, facial expressions
- ♥ Enjoys dictating or recording stories, poems, etc.
- ♥ May dictate or record stories to accompany pictures
- ♥ Begins labeling & using titles
- ♥ Plays with words & letters
- ♥ Often orients letters correctly
- ♥ Associates more letters than before with sounds
- ♥ Writes letter strings
- ♥ Feels confident to "write by myself"
- ♥ Enjoys writing
- ♥ Adds details that might have been overlooked earlier
- ♥ Uses words or pictures to express personal feelings

```
I lu mom n Dad

No Yes en Dad moM

T heoroL The Thing

ABC De FG hij kL mNo Pq

rstu vw xyz

moMiwoairo trBohoPr
```

Stage 3:
Confident Experimentation

The student

- ♥ Feels more confident imitating environmental print
- ♥ Writes more
- ♥ Experiments with letters & rudimentary words
- ♥ Shows greater attention to detail in letters & prephonetic words
- ♥ Attempts longer expressions (two or more words)
- ♥ Shows more awareness of conventions of print: spaces between words, spaces between lines, use of capital letters, up-down orientation, left-right orientation, use of punctuation
- ♥ Begins using some capital letters, which may be randomly placed or used on words of personal importance
- ♥ Begins to experiment with punctuation, though not necessarily appropriately placed

me and my hors.

I can lift my horsi fee. I can ride Him.
I can kick Him. I Love Him. I think He
is neat. I can go beahid Him.

Emily
Grade 1

Stage 4:
Moving Toward Independence

The student

- ♥ Becomes a keen observer of environmental print
- ♥ Feels increasing confidence copying & using environmental print
- ♥ Enjoys writing words, phrases, & short sentences on his or her own
- ♥ Expands oral stories & all-about essays
- ♥ Enjoys drawing pictures—then creating accompanying text
- ♥ Writes longer, more expansive text or uses pictures in a series
- ♥ Asks more questions about writing
- ♥ Asks questions about conventions
- ♥ Includes more conventions of writing in own text, including periods, question marks, commas, quotation marks, capital letters—which may or may not be appropriately placed
- ♥ Likes to share—may ask others to read text

this story is abut my Ant's dog he is special. I im going to rite abut a dog that is special to me. the dog that im reteing abut is specal to me becase I play fech wit him and let him chase me around all the time and I get to tak him for a wok sum time but I can't do that no mor becase I don't see him no mor.

Stage 5:
Expanding & Adding Detail

The student

♥ Writes more—multiple sentences up to a paragraph or more
♥ Experiments with different forms: lists, recipes, how-to papers, all-about essays, stories, poems, descriptions, journals, notes
♥ Begins using some conventions (spaces between words, capitals, periods, title at the top) with growing consistency
♥ Shows increasing understanding of what a sentence is
♥ Adds more detail to both pictures & text
♥ Expresses both ideas & feelings purposefully & forcefully through pictures & text
♥ Shows increasing confidence experimenting with inventive spelling—especially if encouraged
♥ Aims for correct spelling, & uses environment as a resource
♥ Shows expanding vocabulary—especially if inventive spelling is encouraged
♥ Increasingly uses writer's vocabulary to ask questions or discuss own writing—especially if traits are taught

PRIMARY WRITERS' VERY OWN SCORING GUIDE

Jollee Ellis of McNeil Canyon Elementary School, Kenai Peninsula Borough School District, Homer, Alaska has developed a scoring guide that even the very youngest writers can learn to use by matching their writing to that which appears in one of 11 various levels of proficiency. (A teacher's key is included to help you interpret what you see.)

Here is Jollee's introduction in her own words ...

*T*his illustration

of the Kenai Peninsula Borough School District's language arts curriculum writing rubric is my way of making this document available to kindergarten and first-grade students in my class. If they are going to be assessed by this rubric, then they should know what it means. I display the 11 posters [for the 11 levels in the scoring guide] in a prominent place in the classroom, easily accessible to students. I teach that putting pen, pencil, marker, or crayon to paper or using a computer or typewriter to communicate an idea is writing, be that writing a picture, scribble, random letters or symbols, invented spelling, or correctly spelled words. Every child has a writing folder, and they write every day from the first day of school. My goals are fluency and self-confidence.

Students are given ample authentic reasons to write throughout the year in every curriculum area. They learn to write for different audiences, including adults and peers. The use of an author's chair gives them opportunities to read their materials to other students and obtain feedback in the form of questions and comments. Small response groups help with the beginning stages of rewriting, expanding their material and editing. This usually does not take place until first grade for most students.

The children have complete ownership of their writing and may choose to accept suggestions or not as they see fit. I never write or correct on children's papers for fear that fluency will be hindered. I do not want students to get the message that they cannot "do it right" because then they will only put down what they think the teacher wants and will only spell words they know are correct. Creativity becomes lost and self-confidence wanes. There will be plenty of time for editing later.

By seeing the progression of fluency on the 11 posters, children feel encouraged to follow their own gains. They may ask me how they can become a 6 or 8. We look at the posters and discuss the difference between their assessed papers and those particular ratings. Often they say that they can do it, or that they want to learn how to jump to the next level. In this way, they learn to take responsibility for their own learning by setting goals.

They derive great satisfaction from the comparison of early papers to their later writings. My experience has been that if children feel they have a "real" reason to write, they need no other encouragement. You need only to get out of their way.

Jollee Ellis
Kenai Peninsula Borough School District
Homer, Alaska

#1

Text not readable yet.

#2

No text.

Reprinted courtesy of Jollee Ellis, Homer, AK

#3
Imitative writing
not readable yet.

#4
The word "love"
with random letters.

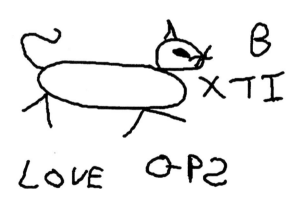

B
X T I

LOVE O P S

Reprinted courtesy of Jollee Ellis, Homer, AK

#5

Beginnings of words we can guess at: " My cat," "pretty," "funny," "frisky," etc. Can't be sure without reader's help!

MCONPTFN
FRISKIE2

#6

" I have a funny kitty."

IHVIFNEKTE

Reprinted courtesy of Jollee Ellis, Homer, AK

#7

" I have a funny cat named
Fluffy. I like her."

I HAV A FAME
CATNAMOFL
AFE ILK HR

#8

" I have a black cat named Midnight.
He's all black with yellow eyes. I
like him."

I hav ablec catna
md mdnit hez ol
blecwth yilo iz I
lik Hm

Reprinted courtesy of Jollee Ellis, Homer, AK

48

#9

"My cat is funny and I like
his feet. They are white and
look funny and I laugh."

MY caT iz fune and
I lik hiz Fet tha
R WHiT and look
funE and i LAF

#10

"I have a funny cat. He runs
after my mom and looks silly. I really
like him. Blackie makes me laugh a lot."

I hav a funne.cat
he runzaftr my
Mom. and Loks
sile I. rele lik
HeM? blace Maks
Me laF alut

Reprinted courtesy of Jollee Ellis, Homer, AK

49

#11

"We got a kitten today that is very cute. She has blue eyes and black and white spots all over. We named her Fluffy because she is soft and furry. I love her oodles."

We got a kiten toda that is vre qut. She has blue,ise and black and white spots ol ovr? We namd her flufy becaws she is soft and fure. I love her oodls.

Reprinted courtesy of Jollee Ellis, Homer, AK

TeaCHeR's KeY To THe 11 LeVels

1. Writer draws or randomly scribbles.
   Reader/viewer can infer no connection to given topic.

2. Draws two-dimensional, profile picture related to specific topic.
   Can retell story about topic/picture.

3. Draws picture about topic.
   Writes with imitative/scribble writing.
   Retells story about topic/picture.

4. Draws picture about topic.
   Writes with random letters, letter strings.
   Copies environmental print.
   May include unrelated sight-word vocabulary.
   Retells story about topic/picture.

5. Draws picture about topic.
   Writes related words using first/last consonants.
   Extends beginning sounds with random strings of letters.
   Copies environmental print.
   Retells story about topic/picture.

6. Draws picture showing beginning proportion, rudimentary detail.
   Writes related words using invented spelling.
   Includes enough letters to make words readable or almost readable
     (with guessing).
   Copies environmental print.
   Retells story about topic/picture.

7. Draws picture showing proportion, some detail, three-dimensional look.
   Writes related words using invented spelling with most consonants, some vowels.
   Writes multiple sentences/phrases.
   Begins using spaces between words.
   Copies environmental print.
   Retells story about topic/picture.

8. Draws picture showing proportion, detail, expression.
   Uses invented spelling with most consonants, some vowels.
   Uses fairly regular spacing between words.
   Writes multiple sentences/phrases.

9. Uses prephonetic and phonetic spelling.
   Writes in sentences.
   Uses multiple sentences.
   Creates text that is readily readable by others.
   Includes many vowel sounds.
   Includes details, not just general ideas.

10. Creates readable text.
    Uses mostly phonetic spelling.
    Writes in multiple sentences.
    Shows detail and complexity of thought.
    Experiments with punctuation.

11. Uses multiple sentences.
    Varies sentence beginnings.
    Speaks with strong personal voice.
    Spelling is mostly phonetic—correct on simple words.
    Continues experimenting with punctuation.
    Uses new words.
    Enriches text with detail and description.

Chapter 4

STUDENT WRITING

I lu mom n Dad
No Yes en Dad mom
TheorolThe Thing
ABC De FG hij kL mNo Pq
restu vw xyz
moMI woairotrBohoPr

Pre-school

I love Mom and Dad

No Yes and Dad Mom

These are all the things [I can write]

ABCDEFGHIJKLMNOPQRSTUVWXYZ

Mom, I want an Aero-Turbo hopper

My dol and me

When I was sick I koont go to scool. my mom gave me a spashl dol. I like the veary mash. this is a very spashl bol to me. if ti got lost I wood de very sad. she is very very very spashl tome me bol.

Grade 1

me and my hors.

I can lift my horsi fee. I can ride Him.
I can kick Him. I Love Him. I think He
is neat. I can go beahid Him.

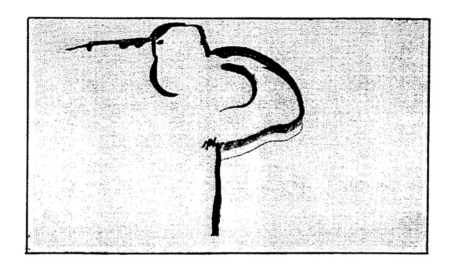

Grade 1

abawot everything

my cat is very very
very very importint thing.
My sicinte very impotint
thing is my Venis Fly trap

Grade 2

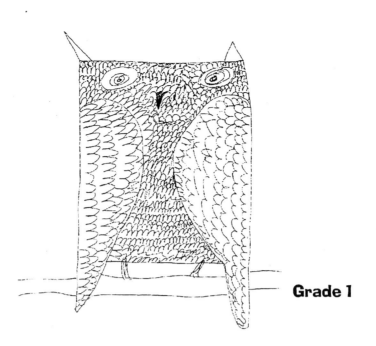

Grade 1

THE GREAT HORNED OWL
There once was a Great Horned Owl
Who thought he was a wonderful fowl.
He flew into a tree
And said "My, oh me!"
Then let out a tremendous howl.

Grade 3

Grade 1

Grade 3

Grade 1

AN ERASER
What can you do with an eraser?
You can erase things.
You can loan it to your best friend.
You can erase your work if you make a mistake.
You can be a judge and stick a pencil in your eraser
to call the court to order.
You can throw it away.
You can erase the past and it will be gone forever.

Grade 3

Grade 2

what is poetry?
  Poetry is moosick
to me on a pees of
paper moosick that
rimes soft moosick
to my ers.

Grade 2

Grade 1

A dog saw an apple tree. He hit the tree, and one apple fell. And the dog ate it.

You're My Special Friend Because ...

Ruff Rack you're my special friend because
When I put up dumb posters you don't laugh.
You like pizza, same as me.
When I get a haircut you don't laugh.
No matter how I look, you don't mind.
When I read to you, you don't get bored.

Ruff Rack you're my Special Friend because
when I am sad you cheer me up.
You always let me yell at you.
You never talk back.
When I think about silly things you never laugh about them.

Ruff Rack you're my Special Friend because
I am sad when we're apart.

Grade 2

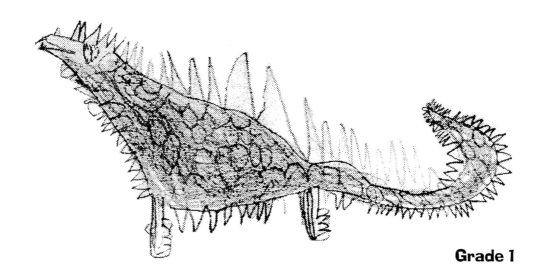

Grade 1

The Werewolf

It was Halloween night. It was dark. It was scary. Everybody had to stay in their houses.

There was a werewolf. He liked to suck blood. He was all hairy and ugly. He snuck in a house.

The next day the police found the house a mess. They finally found a lady in the house. She had a long scratch on her back and she was all shriveled up. Then, as fast as a flash, the werewolf grabbed one of the police and dragged him under the bed. Then he sucked his blood.

The other police ran to get help. This time he came back with a whole troop of police. They searched the house. They found no sign of the werewolf or the policemen.

It was very late so they went to bed.

Grade 2

Apes Over Grapes

I like grapes cause I go apes over grapes
then I pull down the drapes.

Grade 1

TOMATOES ARE BAD

Tomatoes taste terrible
Even though they are bearable.
So don't eat tomatoes
Eat potatoes!

Grade 2

Grade 2

DID YOU NOTICE?

On the following pages are some things you might have noticed about the sample student writings and drawings we've shared in this book. Maybe you also noticed some things we overlooked!

I lu mom n Dad

Very expansive for a preschooler. Really beginning to connect letters to sounds. Using the power of writing to get attention: Mom—I want an Aero-Turbo Hopper! Lots of pride in the writing. Confidence is growing.

Comment: I can read this, Michael! I can tell how much you want that Turbo-Hopper!

My dol and me

Lots of feeling. Developing voice. Good focus—sticks with the topic. Developing sense of sentences. Repetition of "very" shows self-expression.

Comment: I can tell how much your doll means to you! I hope you never lose her. "Special" is a good word for describing things dear to your heart.

me and my hors.

Variety of ideas. Really writing from experience—knows a lot about horses. Uses both picture and text to convey ideas. Enthusiasm. Fairly expanded text. Using inventive spelling well.

Comment: You must trust your horse a lot to lift his feet and walk behind him. I could picture him clearly—great IDEAS!

Heron (picture)

Visually beautiful. Striking. Notice the spare use of lines that creates an especially fluid, impressionistic effect.

Comment: Wow. I'd love this on my mantel. By the way, I noticed you left some parts blank—kind of the way writers don't always tell EVERYTHING. I really like that. What will you draw next?

abowot everything

Interesting choice of topics—cats and Venus flytraps! Nice spacing between words and lines. Very aware of periods. Strong expression of feelings. Beginning awareness of capital letters. Readable spelling—very easy to process. A beginning sense of sequencing; handles two topics nicely.

Comment: Your paper was easy to read and follow. You were the ONLY one who wrote about a Venus flytrap. What an original idea! By the way, I noticed you put a capital V on Venus—how did you know to do that?

Owl (picture)

Lots of detail: Look at all those feathers! This artist has really noticed how feathers are shaped and grouped, too. Interesting proportions and use of geometric shapes. Eyes, tufts, and feet show real awareness of detail.

Comment: I feel as if this owl is staring right through me. There is so much detail here! You have really looked closely at feathers, haven't you? I noticed you used lots of shapes, too—circles, triangles, rectangles. Tell me about that. How long did this take you?

THE GREAT HORNED OWL (poem)

Good rhythm. Intriguing word choice. Very expressive. Use of exclamation point and quotation marks quite sophisticated.

Comment: Your owl has lots of attitude. I like that. You seem to enjoy writing poetry—your voice really comes through.

Dinosaur Monster (picture)

Wonderfully expressive. Strong outlines. Lots of color. Shows emotion, but some humor, too. Creates sense of anticipation in the viewer.

Comment: This dinosaur looks fierce, determined, and full of fight. There's a word for that kind of feeling in a picture: VOICE! Your picture's got it. If you keep writing and drawing like this, everyone will want to read your work!

Bulldozer (picture)

Incredible level of detail. This writer/artist has really looked at bulldozers, machines, earth moving, hard-hats, etc. Expressive, too.

Comment: I can't believe how many things you noticed: the lines in the hat, the little rocks in the earth, the shapes of the treads. Every time I look at your picture I see something new.

Train (picture)

Good proportion on the page. Use of multiple colors. The steam suggests lots of movement and speed, giving the picture more impact and voice.

Comment: I get the feeling of motion when I look at your picture. I love how powerful this train seems—it's got a lot of voice.

An Eraser

Thoughtful—goes well beyond the obvious: "You can erase the past ... ." Whimsical, too. Combines ideas with feelings. Excellent control of conventions, and a nice, rhythmic sound, too.

Comment: I thought erasers were mostly for mistakes. You helped me think of some new ideas. Isn't it funny how a little thing can turn into a big topic? I love it when a writer makes me see something in a new way!

Whale (picture)

Bold, visually striking, well proportioned.

Comment: Have you read Amos and Boris by William Steig? That's what your picture made me think of—the wonderful whale, Boris, who had so much courage he risked his life for his friend. I think you would enjoy the pictures in William Steig's book, too.

What is poetry?

Lyrical, fluent, beautiful. What an ear for language this young writer has. He has wonderful sentence sense, even if he isn't punctuating his sentences yet.

Comment: I read this aloud and it has the most wonderful rhythm and sound. I loved it. Do you like poetry? I think your writing sounds a lot like poetry! Have you read Gary Paulsen's book <u>Dogteam</u>? I think you would love it.

Tree and Dog (picture and story)

Joyful. Whimsical. Good left-right orientation. Good coordination between picture and story. Nice control of sequencing from a very young writer.

Comment: Your picture and your story go together so well. Your story was easy to follow, too. The ending surprised me totally. I never knew dogs ate apples.

You're My Special Friend Because ...

Impressive originality. Wonderful humor, voice. Exceptional detail: e.g., "When I get a haircut you don't laugh." Excellent sentence sense. Good use of simple language to express thoughtful, important ideas.

Comment: You put a lot of thought into this poem. My favorite parts were not laughing about the haircut and not getting bored when someone reads to you out loud. Those are really important qualities in a friend, and they are the kinds of details not everybody thinks of.

Dragon (picture)

Expressive. This dragon looks downright soulful—shy, even. He's got a great tail; the scales and the spikes lend flavor and detail, but it's the face and backward feet that win your heart.

Comment: When I look at this dragon's face, I can't help thinking he might be friendlier than most. Tell me, did you do that on purpose?

The Werewolf

Exceptional sequencing for such a young writer. Fair control over a wide range of details. Expanded text, showing a growing control of fluency, and lots of experimenting with conventions. This writer is paying attention to environmental print. Amazing control of paragraphing. Admittedly violent—but still enthusiastic!

Comment: You sure put together a good Halloween story. What happened to the lady who was "all shriveled up"? Does that mean she died? I was a little surprised everyone went home to bed in the middle of all that action. Did the werewolf go to bed too?

Apes Over Grapes

Short but to the point. Readable, funny.

Comment: Your poem made me laugh. I could tell you had a good time writing it, and I had a good time reading it.

TOMATOES ARE BAD

Hilarious. "Terrible ... [but] bearable." Anyone who's ever wished a tomato were on someone else's plate will appreciate this great poem. Outstanding for this moment of word choice—but also great rhythm and the courage and insight to choose a humble subject and have fun with it.

Comment: I LOVE this poem. "Bearable" was the perfect word!! Perfect. Thanks for writing a poem about the tomato. Who would have thought tomatoes would make such a great topic??

Hummingbird (picture)

Glorious detail. Notice the tail feathers, the shape of the flower, the long bill, the veins in the leaves.

Comment: Your picture made me think I should look more closely at hummingbirds and flowers both. What details! You even captured the tail feathers on that hummingbird, and the veins in the leaves.

Every piece of student work is special in some way—in detail, in feeling, in topic selection, or whatever. The trick is to teach ourselves to notice the specialness—to see with new eyes—and to respond to content and feeling first.

A DIVERSE COLLECTION OF STUDENT WORK

As you look over the student writing and art samples on the next few pages, watch for details and insights (ideas), sense of balance and sequence (organization), individuality, flavor and emotional tone (voice), careful and original word selection (word choice), rhythm and flow (sentence fluency), and skill in borrowing both traditional and creative layout and structure from environmental print (conventions).

Really try to look inside each piece. Notice which students are having fun, taking risks, trying something a little unusual.

Ask yourself each time, "What comment could I make to help this writer see his/her strengths with new eyes?"

A Diverse Collection of student work, featuring ...

- **Stories**
- **Adventures & narrow escapes**
- **Descriptions**
- **Sketches**
- **Reflective responses to literature (<u>Leo the Late Bloomer</u>)**
- **Imaginative pieces (pretending to be something <u>other than a person</u>)**

What strengths do you see within? How could you help these students to see what they do well?

My holladay traditions are opening christamas presents we take tuns opening the presents my mom always tells me to save the presents rapers but I open them as fast as I can I don't care how I open them I just go psyco untill they are open

Joel
Grade 2

The Foot Ball

It was a hot day. We were driving to the Huskey game. The Huskeys were playing them self because it was a Spring Scrtimmage after the game you got to go down on the field. so we stoped at a sport shop on the way, and I got a leather football. Afte the game was over I wnet down on the fild with my football and a pen. I went to almost evey player and asked tem to atograp it.

It was neat. I met almost every player on the team. And they all atograft my football! I even got the coach to sine it.

It was a grate day now some of the players are pro some of the players who went pro are Nopolen Kuffman he went to the Raders. Steve Eatman went to the Colts their where alot more but I don't know what teams they went to. But I know some more Huskey's will become pro some day.

Joel
Grade 2

this story is abut my Ant's dog he is special. I im going to rite abut a dog that is special to me. the dog that im riteing abut is specal to me becase I play fech wit him and l et him chase me around all the time and I get to tak him for a wok sum time but I can't do that no mor becase I don't see him no mor.

Ignacio
Grade 2

Someone/Something

My mom is special to me because she makes my lunch. And she gets me my stuf like my school supliys. She takes me to my faverit resteront. And my mom is special to me because she plays games with me. And she got my staryor. and she got me to ride in the limizing for my brthday.

Joey
Grade 2

My Dad Playing Softball

When my Dad was playing Softball he was in the outfield anther guy on my Dad's team he pitched the ball the other team hit the ball in the outfall. Chuk and my Dad were going after the ball they both collided into each other. The ball hited my dads nose my Dad was dazed. The blood gushed out of his nose. My step mom had to take him to the Hospital. His nose was broken. He felt miserable. It was a emergency so they had to put some string in his nose and pull on it to straiten it out. My Dad felt really panic stricken when the nurse pulled on his nose. He yelled loudly in the emergency room. Chuk also had a black eye for a week. Hey, I wonder why they call it softball.

Steven
Grade 3

My favorate meal is enchaladae casarol. It is about five or six diffrent kinds of burritos in a dish. My mom usually cooks it in the summer time on hot nights. When my mom, my dad and my brother sit down at the table and we have a nice meal together. I love when we sit down togeter and when wher done I am foll. Those enchaladas are so filling and tasty.

Andy
Grade 3

The way I enjy speding free time is drawing. I really like drawing decause it is fun and just like a book you can go anywhere with it. I mostly like drawing dogs, trees, log cabin, and Pet stores.

I like animals alot. I want to be a vetraneran when I grow up. So I disided to draw pet stores and animals. I lik to draw.

Christina
Grade 3

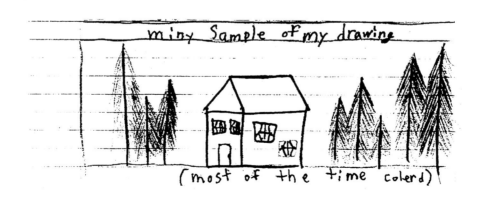
miny Sample of my drawing
(most of the time colerd)

My favorite snack on a cold winter day is chickin noodle soup and hot coco with marshmelows as white as snow in it and the marshmelows were as flufy as a pilow. the first reson I like that stuff for a winter snak is... I like the marshmelows. the second reson is I lik the choclot. the lst reson is I like the tast of choclot and chickin. The end

Bye-bye

Grade 2

When I had my accident on a bike

When I was 5 years old I couldn't wait to try new thugs. Like when I accidently broke my mom's car windo. I lied that a 9 year old did it.

My grandma has an Pee Wee Herman bike its very old. I was riding it whith my cosen and my grandpa was vido taping us. It was my turn when Out of the sky I ran into the fence and luckaly he didn't get me on tape.

I ran into the house with a bloody face because the kuick stand was lose. It was Wenesday. I hope you don't let It happen to you.

Shawn
Grade 3

Selina and the Hunters

Has anyone ever asked you what you think its like in the jungle, or it you ever want to be a lion and disappear into the jungle. Well you don't need to because I'm can tell you about the jungle right now.

I'm an Orangutan monkey named Selina I love my home here in the jungle and I have many stories to tell you. Which one should I tell you. Ah yes I have the most perfect story to tell you.

One day I was clutched tight between my mothers side and her arm as she swing form limb to limb. When all of a sudden the loud fast sound of a bullet came scraping through the ski hissing through the wind that was not there and disturbing all the animals. My mother stood still in her steps and clutched me tighter.

"Mama what was that?"

"Nothing" she said with fright in her voice. Then came another bullet shooting trough the sky swallowing up the peace gulp by gulp and eating up the quiet.

Not much after that came a rush of animals in a big group like a swarm of bees.

"Krana" my mother said to another Orangutan "Is anyone hurt" "no but soon to be." "They have 10 elephants on the run and a whole bunch of other animals." "by the time these hunters are gone the whole jungle will be extinct".

"We have to stop theme said my mother." "No" said Krana. "Why not?"

"Because!" "Because why?"

"Whey almost got Shikiwa."

"Where is he?" "Home safe with Lala. Thank goodness" said my mother. "But he's safe now so lets go." "We have to start thinking of other animals and not are self." "All right" said Krana.

"Mama don't leave me" I said tears filling my eyes. "Shh don't cry all be back soon I swear." "OK" I said wiping my eyes. "Good luck" I said "you're my good luck charm" she said smiling. Then she kissed me and left.

After I had listened to a story I said to Lala "You look very tired grandfather you need to rest."

"I ca-" "Shh my dear old man and rest." "Me and Shkiwa will be good." I finally got him to go to sleep. Then I told Shkiwa if Lala woke up not to let him know I wasn't there and I left. The jungle was not warm or welcome but quiet and queer.

As I walked I heard a million bullets. When I went to rest in the sun I saw my mother and Krana resting there too.

As I sat in the grass I heard my mother say that they were never going to tell all the animals on the east side of the jungle to meet back there when the 20th bullet shot. I can help then I thought.

The first animals I found were a family of tigers. I told them what ever animals they find to tell them that they all need to meet in the sunny spot when the 20th bullet shot. "All right" they said.

When I had told all the animals on the east side I waited for the 20th bullet shot and 2 as many animals came my mother was so surprised. When she saw me she said "Selina whats going on?" "I don't have time to expand" I said "we have to save the jungle if its still worth saving."

We got all the animals into a big line and counted to 3. Then we all ran across the jungle. When we got to the hunters they were just about to shoot two elephants when they saw us they dropped there guns and ran to other way. I hope you liked the story.

Soren
Grade 3

77

RESPONSES TO LITERATURE

I've bloomed.
Before I couldn't read.
Now I can read.
Tiye my shows.
I can mack lunch

Shayna
Grade 1

I've bloomed.
Befor I couldn't reid and I couldnt do math. Now I
can reid and do math. Now I now how to do my hare.

Alyssa
Grade 1

I've bloomed.
Before I couldn't riet and reid I evein kedt cout'n you sey tos av
theys are hard to do so now you now so if you get in trubl it is not
your folt sum times.

Garrett
Grade 1

I've bloomed.
Before I couldn't read or right or double digit. Now I can do
double digit and read and right and color and math.

Jessie
Grade 1

**Responses to <u>Leo the Late Bloomer,</u> by Robert Kraus. 1971. Harper Collins.
ISBN #0-87807-042-7.**

"IF I WERE SOMETHING OTHER THAN A PERSON..."

I am a nice storybook

I was made in Portland Oregon. One day I was bought by a littl mean boy named zack. A week later. The mean boy read all of my storys so the thrugh me away in the stinky chrash can. The next day a nother boy named Sameal. He was a nede boy he had no famly at all. He notest me in the stinky garbeage. He took me out of the stinky gargege. A week or tow he finished with all of my stores. But he did not throw me away. H cept reading my storys over and over. And that is my story. The End.

Ashley
Grade 2

How I got To be a pencil.

I am a populer tree. I live in a rain forest. I have many freinds. One day I was resting in the warm sun. Then I saw a short man whith a Big chain saw. Befor I knew it I was in a blue truck. Then I was taken out. I went into a Big machine. When I came out I was a little smaller than before. Next I was put on brown table in a big room. There were brushes and bottles and odds and ends. I was having so much fun I dindt notice that I had Been carved really thin. Then I was painted: pink, blue, Green, and purple. Next the short man glued a Peace of rubber. It was painted with "tie-die." Then he ran a flat machine over me. I was smooth now. Then I was put on a sort wight shelf. And in ten seconds flat a tall thin Girl picked me up and put me on a counter. Next I was put in a wight desk. Years passed. I had one inch of led left. My paint was gone. but I was still usful.

Caitie
Grade 2

80

If I Were a Roller Coaster

If I were a roller coasater. I could have peaple in my back. I could go up a steap hill and down. But the bad thing is when the peaple get out of my back and go out of the fare. The other thing is that I a have to be put away till the next day. But if I were a roller coaster I would make people screame. That's what I'd do. The End

Alyssa
Grade 2

Pencil

I am a wakeiy pencil with funnky desinens. I do hard arithmetics for little grlis and little boys. I write really ugly, fast and sometimes net, slow. I not only have funnky desinens but my eraser is really net with zig zags all over it. And I do everthing! This is the funnky part how I was made frist I came from a old and very big tree. I got mad into a round little funnky shap of cardar wood. Then they cut a little hole in the middle of my funnky shap and put a funnky black thing so I could write it was called led. Then they colord me and put this funnky eraser on of the top of the medle part on my top. And that is a funnky way to make a pencil. I get smaller and my desines go away and all that is left is my wakiy eraser.

Laura
Grade 2

The Vase.

Once I was a pice of sharp and ponted pice of glass, in the smelly dirty dump and then the nice workers who wrok at the very pretty fanciy Vace Shop said "Hey look at that pice of sharpend ponted big pice of glass we could use that". "defenetly". Said another one. So the took me and made a butoful vase out of me and paited me unitl I was Very pretty !! I sat there for 3 weeks talking to the rest of the very pretty vases. Ten one satay afternoon a nice four person family came in and walked around for a while and ten they came over to the butaful vases, we all don't look alike. They almost picked up my best pretty friend, but they did not, they picked up me !!! And bought me !!! from then on I belonged to the Schrag's. They always have flowers in me so I always have company to talk to. The End

Katie
Grade 2

Once I was a tree. A clook maker cote me down. He stared to carve me into a clook he did dsinse he got nuts and bolts on me he put to hans on me. I than he siade a good clook I was rite yes! I wint o a boot I sald from Origon to cina then they trride to sall me. No butte wanted me. So the guy on the boot bot me. I wint a rond the hole in their wared. The boot and me made good frins we were happy tell we thot we wood drown. But we just landed on a beach The end

Aaron
Grade 2

I want Mrs Hudson to have a boy because then I can make a new friend.

by Rendon

Mrs. Moore on your birthday you should . . . take a walk alone.

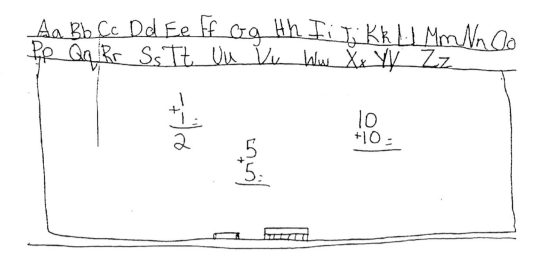

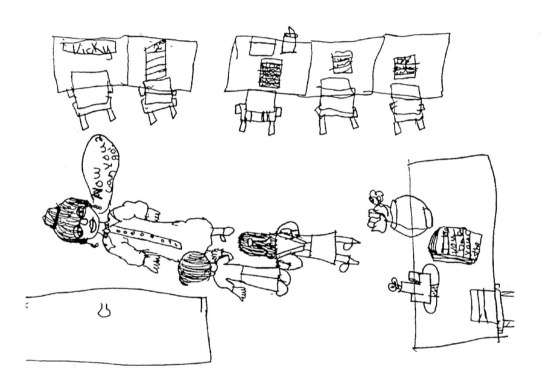

I like to write about class rooms because there are children and many facts about class rooms and many facts can get you a great grade.

Zaneta
Grade 3

ZANETA, GRADE THREE: SELF-PORTRAIT

Wherever we look in time or place,

we see our children and our ancestors forming identical configurations. We have not discovered why this is so, only that it is, and that it is important because our built world is constructed on the principles of logical relationships our children and our ancestors realize.

In these artifacts we can see the human mind and its ability to express relationships of forms, a unique human birthright.

Sylvia Fein
First Drawings: Genesis of Visual Thinking, 137

Chapter 5

PRIMARY WRITING PROCESS

How does the writing process look at

PRIMARY LEVEL?

Read on for a quick summary,

followed by a more indepth look.

WRITING PROCESS: PRIMARY VERSION

1. Prewriting
- ☺ Experiencing/exploring
- ☺ Thinking
- ☺ Discussing
- ☺ Drawing a picture
- ☺ Brainstorming together

2. Drafting
- ✐ Writing
- ✐ Drawing
- ✐ Verbally composing

3. Sharing
- ☺ With the teacher
- ☺ With one other student
- ☺ In a small group
- ☺ With the class
- ☺ With someone at home

4. Revising
Closing your eyes … seeing & feeling & living it again … asking yourself if you want to add or change anything

5. Beginning Editing
- ☺ Is my name on the paper? (a date?)
- ☺ Did I put a title on if I want one?
- ☺ Did I leave spaces between words?
- ☺ Did I leave any words out?

6. Additional editing for experienced writers

✏ Did I use capitals to begin sentences?
✏ Did I use capitals on names?
✏ Did I use periods to end sentences?
✏ Did I use question marks to show which sentences are questions?
✏ Did I use other punctuation marks I need to ask about?
✏ Did I use my best spelling to help my reader?

> ✏ ADD other editing skills as appropriate, ONE AT A TIME!

7. Bringing it to closure

☺ Post the work
☺ Take it home
☺ Put it in a working folder
☺ Put it in a portfolio
☺ Mark down that it was completed
☺ Reflect on the work

An expanded discussion of these steps follows.

89

PRIMARY
WRITING PROCESS

It is much less important to go systematically through the steps and stages of the writing process than to help primary writers understand that writing is thinking, and because it is thinking, it (a) takes time, and (b) sometimes changes. This change, which is up to the writer, is called revision. More about this in a moment. Let's begin at the beginning, with experience ... life itself!

✎ PREWRITING

Writers need something to write about. Surprise! Not all writers have someone willing, able, or motivated to assign writing topics to them. They must hunt up their own. Sometimes, it is good for our young writers to do this too. Other times, of course, we want them to write on something in particular, but often we assign writing more out of habit than out of need.

How do writers come up with their own topics? First, by being curious about life. Don't hesitate to talk about this very directly with your young writers: Curious people have more (usually) to write about, and find writing easier because they are interested in everything. "I have nothing to write about" really does mean "I haven't looked closely enough at my own experience to discover all that I could write about." If you are buried in Nintendo or television, it will be hard to think of ideas outside that world. But if you allow yourself to experience a bigger slice of life, you may begin noticing things:

☺ How spiders spin their webs
☺ How frogs swim
☺ How the pavement smells after a rain
☺ How people always cluster into the middle seats at a theater
☺ How long baby kittens keep their eyes closed
☺ How "express lines" at the grocery store never move

Ask your writers to keep track of what they notice in the world around them, and even (for those who are willing) to keep a journal about it. One-word entries or picture entries are fine!

Also ask them to think about
☺ What worries them
☺ What intrigues them
☺ What makes them angry
☺ What makes them excited or happy

Personal response to life is the stuff of good writing. Virtually every novel or picture book is based on a problem resolved, a difficult situation overcome, a question posed and answered. Of course not all writing is narrative or fiction. So, what writers wonder about often becomes the focus of their research:

👍 How dangerous is lightening, really?
👍 Would a rat bite if cornered?
👍 Do boa constrictors make good pets?
👍 What is the best paying job in America? Why?

Ask them to pose questions, and write them down. Or, if they're not ready to write, you can make a list. Later, share the questions back, and so a simple "research" paper, for which students find one "person who might know," pose the question, and write the answer through text or pictures. Gathering information is part of prewriting, too!

TALKING HELPS
Encourage students to talk to one another early in the process, to ask, "What is your favorite writing topic? How do you get ideas for writing? How do you find information?"

LISTS ARE GOOD, TOO
Brainstorm lists of details or questions. A second-grade teacher friend was planning to take her students on a field trip to the beach, and used the event as an opportunity for informal research. Her students formed groups of four, then each group chose one topic (the starfish, the sea urchin, etc.). They brainstormed four questions about their topic, and used their time on the field trip to answer their questions:

* How big are starfish?
* How many arms do starfish have?
* What happens when you touch a starfish? Are they shy? Aggressive?
* What colors are starfish?

This activity helped writers think like readers. This is important. It is impossible to be a writer without also being a reader. You have to know how it feels to be truly satisfied with what you write, and to be deeply unsatisfied because the writer didn't tell you enough or used words you could not understand. From those experiences comes the beginning of understanding of what it takes to write well.

WHAT WORKS FOR YOU?

What prewriting strategies do YOU use yourself? Let your writers see you in action, whether you compose, draw, make lists, talk out loud to yourself or someone else, make word webs, or whatever. Let them SEE you. Don't try to be wonderful. Just be a writer.

✎ DRAFTING

For experienced writers, this usually means quickly getting ideas onto the page, via pen, pencil, or word processing program. Drafting is a generative phase, when we want writers to momentarily stifle the editor in their minds, and let the ideas flow! Let 'er rip!

For beginning writers, it's not quite that simple. Fluency comes with time. We can help by (1) providing realistic chunks of time (enough to allow the ideas to emerge, not so much that beginners become exhausted), and (2) allowing writing to take many forms, depending on what is comfortable for the writer. This might include scribbles or imitative text, copying from environmental print, pictures of all kinds, labeling, writing conventional text, or composing orally (as part of a group activity, or as personal dictation).

Writing truly is more than putting words on a page. It is thinking of an idea, and finding a way to share it in a way that informs, entertains, or persuades someone else. The thinking and planning part of writing can often occur as students plan a series of pictures, as they label parts of a poster, or as they help you compose a letter to the gas company asking why rates are so high. Give your writers real-life purposes for writing, and they will surprise you with their creativity and resourcefulness.

✐ SHARING

Do you like to share your writing by reading it aloud? Lots of people do not! They may be shy, or may be afraid of sharing something as personal as writing with no guarantees anyone will like it or praise it. Is sharing really that important? Eventually, probably, yes. The reason for this is that most of the writing we do in our lives (personal journals aside) is for an audience, and one of the ways we gain a true measure of our success as writers is by judging the impact our writing has upon the intended audience. But what about the student who finds this hard?

TRY ONE OF THESE THINGS ...

☺ Sharing your own writing. Be the first to jump in the pool. Be casual about it. Keep your sharing short, and you can do it often, showing students that sharing can be a good experience if you're among friends.

☺ Talk about ways to respond when someone shares. A thank you is always appropriate. But what kinds of comments are helpful? "I liked it" is nice, but not as helpful as "I could picture your room," which is specific. "I didn't like it" is not helpful, and could hurt a writer's feelings, while naming a specific problem ("I did not know what happened to the dog at the end") is often <u>very</u> helpful. It tells the writer, "Be a little more clear next time." Encourage students to begin their comments with "I," not with "You." "You" comments are often criticisms; "I" comments express a specific reader's problem that the writer can work on solving next time. Above all, encourage support for the writer. Listening attentively is one way to show support. Writers need to feel the environment is safe for sharing.

☺ Let sharing be short. Writers can tell about a picture. They can share a new title, just the first line, just the ending. It isn't always necessary to share the whole thing.

☺ How about sharing a little of the process? Writers can tell the story of how they came up with their ideas, how they got information, how they thought of a particular title, how long the writing took, who helped with editing, one thing they've gotten better at.

Of course, many primary writers love sharing more than any other part of the writing process. Great! Writing is celebrational, after all!

✏ REVISING

Uh-oh. Here we go. Isn't this where writing ceases to be fun, and begins to be a kind of torture? **YES!** Ha—just kidding. It's all in how we approach it. Here, for instance, is one approach that often works less than well:

OK, everybody, remember those great Thanksgiving papers we wrote yesterday? Let's get them out and revise them.

Yuck. Time to go home and pull weeds.

Why? Why is revision so repulsive? For one thing, many primary students have trouble enough getting the copy written in the first place. They're still working on motor skills, spacing, balance, margins, letter orientation, and dozens of other things which come naturally and automatically to older writers. Even if they're working on a computer, redoing everything can sound huge, overwhelming, and generally fun-free. Besides, why would we do over something we just finished? Wasn't finishing the <u>goal</u>? What would you think if you drove all day to get to San Francisco, only to have someone say, "Well, good beginning on your driving there. Hey, that leg through Northern California was one of your best yet. You're really getting it. Now, just head on back to your starting point and give it another shot, and I know your driving is going to be a <u>lot</u> better this time! When you get back here we'll talk about what you've learned" ??? Would it feel worth it? Would you see the point?

Like most of us, primary writers want to either (1) rest from the road for awhile, or (2) drive somewhere <u>else</u>. Good. "Revision" in the sense of learning things about your writing can often work just as well if not better on the draft of the future.

MODEL IT

This does not mean we shouldn't talk about revision, though, or show students how it looks. Did you ever see any of your teachers revise anything? I did not. In fact, I never saw a teacher write anything other than lesson plans, brief notes, and comments on students' work. I did not <u>ever</u> see a teacher write or revise a report, story, poem, research paper, editorial, film or book review, or persuasive essay.

It is easier to do what you have seen. Isn't it easier to drive a car once you've seen someone do it? Or swim? Or dance? Everything is simpler if you have a picture of it in your head. Let your students see you revise. If you revise a poem or letter, talk about it. Tell them how and why you revised, and share the revised version so they can hear the difference. When we share this process with students, we say to them, revision is not fixing what you got wrong. Revision is using your power as a writer.

The secret? <u>Model more than you demand</u>. Show them how it looks, but do not require it. You may be surprised how many will want to try what they have seen you do.

96

In order to help children to develop as writers, we need to share in the writing process by being writers ourselves. By providing demonstrations of writing in action, by being partners in the creating process, we do more to help children figure out how to be writers themselves than all of our correcting of their "mistakes" can ever hope to accomplish.

Judith Newman

The Craft of Children's Writing

WALK THEM THROUGH IT

Walk students through the revision process with this simple exercise.

Picture yourself in your favorite place on earth. Got it? Now, focus on one thing close enough to touch. Take a good look at it. Now, describe what you see. (Students can describe the item with a picture, or text, or a combination of the two. Allow 10 minutes or so for students' descriptions.)

Now, put yourself right back in that same place. Close your eyes if it helps you concentrate. Take another look at the thing you described. Do you notice anything you did not see the first time? Put your hand out and touch it. How does it feel? Listen. Listen hard. Be really still. What do you hear? What are the smells you notice?

Now ... open your eyes and look again at your description. Is there anything you'd like to add you did not think of the first time?

This exercise helps young writers see revision for what it truly is—seeing it again, taking another look. This exercise, like the modeling of revision, reinforces the notion that revision is power, the writer's way of owning and taking charge of the writing. It is not a penalty imposed by others.

As writers become older and more adept, we do not want to dictate to them how or even whether they should revise. We want, rather, to give them a good and thoughtful response, based on a careful reading of their text, and then allow them to do with that information what they will.

WHAT REVISION LOOKS LIKE

Revision takes many forms. Adding information is one of the earliest forms of revision for beginning writers, and many primary writers may have difficulty going beyond this step (till grade 3, 4 or so). Given time, young writers will also experiment with moving text around, adding larger amounts of detail, saying things in a new way, playing with time or other organizational structures and, finally, taking things out. OUCH! That's the one that hurts. So hard the first time. Too hard for many primary writers. (Be honest. Isn't it often hard for us, too?)

✏ EDITING

The chapter on "Teaching Traits to Primary Writers" includes <u>many</u> suggestions for teaching editing to primary writers. The key is really encouraging young writers to do their own editing, and providing instruction in editing skills, including the use of proofreaders' marks for students who are ready (those writing sentences or extended phrases).

Keep in mind that much as we might like to think otherwise, correcting students' work and teaching editing are **NOT** the same thing. Correcting, while time consuming and even sometimes exhausting, is not instructional for students because <u>they are not the ones doing it</u>. It often looks instructional, but it is a shortcut to true editing instruction, and it does not work.

In an editing conference, then, I begin by celebrating what the student has done, and then I teach one or two items.

Lucy McCormick Calkins
The Art Of Teaching Writing, New Edition, 304

It is important that the editing system in our classrooms does not put extraordinary demands on writers who have severe problems. If these children know they must find every single misspelled word in a dictionary, they will write with safe words, choosing *big* when they wanted to say *enormous*.

Lucy McCormick Calkins
The Art Of Teaching Writing, New Edition, 301

When I Had a Bad Day
When I woke up I fell out of bed and when I got drest I poot my shert on backward.

Steven
Grade 3

What **does** work is to put students in charge of their own editing, systematically increasing the complexity of what we hold them responsible for. This is empowering to students, and it is instructional. What do you need to make it happen?

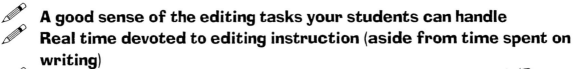 A good sense of the editing tasks your students can handle

Real time devoted to editing instruction (aside from time spent on writing)

Plenty of environmental print that clearly, boldly, & in **LARGE** print reflects the conventions you are teaching

A **BIG** poster of proofreaders' marks

Smaller copies of proofreaders' marks to hand out to students & parents

Very short, very focused editing lessons (Some examples are provided at the conclusion of the section titled "Beginning Editing.")

✏ BRINGING IT TO CLOSURE

This step can include anything that feels like a good ending, from posting work in the classroom to putting it into a portfolio. It might mean taking things home, or checking off that they're completed. So much depends on the classroom routine familiar to and workable for you and your students. Here are some quick suggestions, generously shared with me by a number of primary teachers, for helping things go smoothly.

PUBLISHING

Do NOT feel compelled to publish everything. It's exhausting for everyone, and completely unrealistic. No one publishes everything she or he writes. (Well, maybe James Michener comes close. Maybe. But still.) Encourage students to be selective about what goes all the way through the process. This means not everything will need to be edited, either. What on earth is the point? If we're trying to increase students' editing skills, we can do that more effectively and more systematically on structured practice that does not involve their own text. In time, given regular editing practice, their skills as proofreaders and editors will transfer very nicely to their own work, with amazing results.

If we insist they edit their own work, we'll end up doing it anyway. Is that what we want? What, exactly, do we have in mind to do with all these little edited pieces of writing? Which brings us to ...

FINAL EDITING

Believe it or not, for some people, this is a favorite step in the writing process. It was one of mine. Honest. I made a living for many years as an editor (and writer), and even now I love it when someone says, "Here—would you proof this?" You will have students who love it, too. Encourage them, as they become proficient, to take an active role in the writing process, and to help others with those proofreading skills they <u>really</u> have down. Be honest, though. It's bad enough to have your text ripped apart by a competent (or creative) editor (sometimes they write better than you do, and that can be helpful or annoying, depending on your mood); but to be overhauled by someone who cannot spell or punctuate is neither helpful nor morale boosting.

Do final editing (beyond what the student asks about in a conference, or something important you wish to point out for instructional purposes) only on pieces which will be published. This, too, is true to real life. Manuscripts for published books are scrutinized by several pairs of well-trained eyes before the book hits the shelves, but no one in the real world of publishing expects this kind of attention to be paid to a draft not slated for publication. It's too time consuming. So, choose wisely, then ...

(1) Let the writer herself go as far as she can with her piece.
(2) Provide skilled editing help (you, a trained and skillful parent, or a trained and skillful older student).
(3) Ensure that plenty of resources (computer spell checker, dictionaries, handbooks of various kinds, posters, checklists) are available as references for you, the editor, and the writer.
(4) Encourage the writer, if she wishes, to not only look over, but to <u>approve</u> the final editing (and to change some things back if she prefers). In real life (thank goodness) writers do have this option. In real life, the writer owns the writing, start to finish, and the editor is her assistant. In the world of the classroom, the opposite is often true.
(5) Give credit for any and all work done on editing on the cover or title page of the publication: Written by _____, Edited by _____ .

ENCOURAGE REFLECTION

Oh, no—not MORE writing??!! Well, not necessarily. Students <u>can</u> write self-reflections, certainly, and often do when they choose something to go into a portfolio. But they can also meet in their writing groups just to talk for five minutes about what each has learned, or what they feel proud of in their publications. The process of looking back, reflecting, and asking, "What did I learn?" is really what is important. This is so, by the way, whether the writing finds its way into a portfolio or not. Portfolios help honor students' work by preserving what we and what they treasure. But the real learning comes from choosing those works which are important enough to save, plus reflecting on the writer's journey.

This is why we assess: to learn. If these children can't talk easily about texts, they will have a hard time being critical readers of their own or anyone else's writing.

Lucy McCormick Calkins
The Art Of Teaching Writing, New Edition, 326

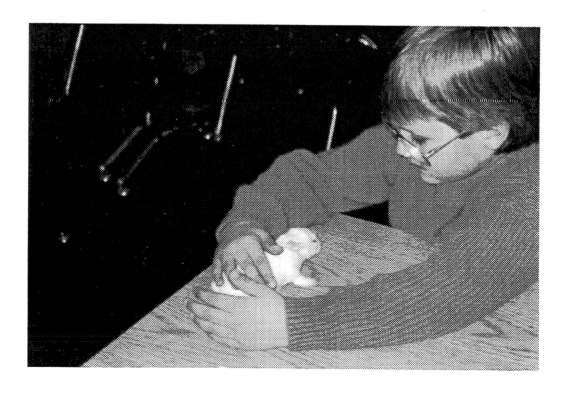

103

STUDENT-LED CONFERENCES

Let the student take the lead in identifying his or her strengths and growth areas. If students complete the self-assessment continuum on the following page first, the conference part will be shorter and easier. These criteria, by the way, were all developed by primary students working with their teachers. You could use all or some of these—or you and your students could develop your own list. (Your list does NOT have to be this long, either!) Remember that the process of putting together criteria is what teaches and encourages students to think like writers.

Shared courtesy of **Rhonda Hunt**
and **Jill Harper**
Primary Teachers
Douglas County Schools
Minden, Nevada

GOOD WRITER TRAITS

Name:_____

Date:_____

1. I choose good words in my writing.
   1   2   3   4   5

2. I have good ideas in my writing.
   1   2   3   4   5

3. I have good organization in my writing. I stay on topic and it all goes together.
   1   2   3   4   5

4. My sentences read very fluently.
   1   2   3   4   5

5. You can hear my voice in my writing.
   1   2   3   4   5

6. I use conventions properly in my writing.
   1   2   3   4   5

7. I plan my writing before I write.
   1   2   3   4   5

8. I make sure my pieces have all the parts.
   1   2   3   4   5

9. I have interesting characters in my stories.
   1   2   3   4   5

10. I revise my work.
    1   2   3   4   5

11. I edit with a friend.
    1   2   3   4   5

12. I write for myself and for others.
    1   2   3   4   5

13. I like to read my writing to others.
    1   2   3   4   5

Strengths: Growth areas:

My main strengths are:

My main areas of growth are:

KEYS TO CONFERRING WITH PRIMARY WRITERS

1. Let the writer hold the pencil.

2. Keep the conference SHORT. A minute or two is often plenty.

3. Respond to CONTENT first. Respond much the way you would if you received a postcard from a good friend.

4. Let the student do <u>most</u> of the talking.

5. Ask the student (ahead of time, so she can prepare) to kick things off with a question.

6. Ask WHY. "Why did you use an exclamation point here? Why did you choose this title?"

7. Resist thinking for the writer. Let the writer make decisions about what to do next.

8. Resist the urge to "fix" things. Focus on the writer and the process, not on creating a perfect product.

9. Revising? Ask the writer, "Close your eyes for a minute and see it again. See if there's anything you didn't think of the first time."

10. Hold editing conferences separately; keep writers focused on ideas and voice for as long as you can.

11. In editing conferences, let the writer take the lead, hold the pencil, guide the conference, and ask specific questions. Don't just **CORRECT THINGS**. It is better to leave some things undone and let the writer tell you what she knows and what she needs to know.

12. Praise the writer for her work <u>on the process</u>, not for the piece of writing—YET!! Too much praise too soon may encourage the writer to stop working.

Let the writer teach you.

WRITING DO'S & DON'TS

DO ...

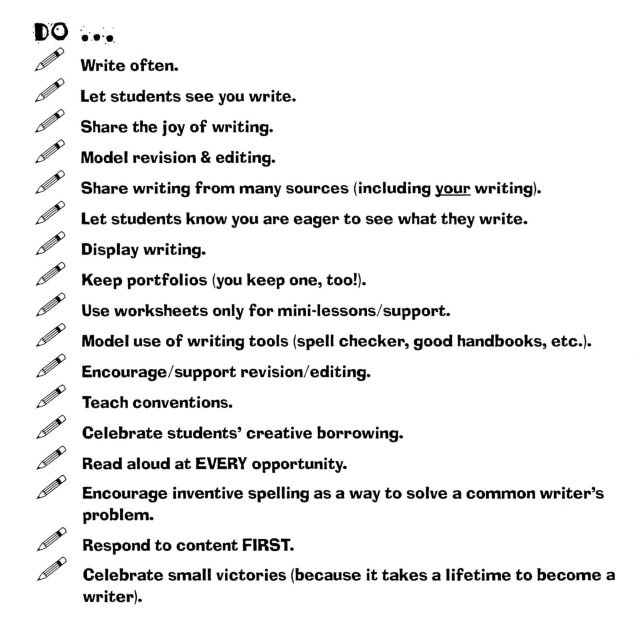

- Write often.

- Let students see you write.

- Share the joy of writing.

- Model revision & editing.

- Share writing from many sources (including <u>your</u> writing).

- Let students know you are eager to see what they write.

- Display writing.

- Keep portfolios (you keep one, too!).

- Use worksheets only for mini-lessons/support.

- Model use of writing tools (spell checker, good handbooks, etc.).

- Encourage/support revision/editing.

- Teach conventions.

- Celebrate students' creative borrowing.

- Read aloud at EVERY opportunity.

- Encourage inventive spelling as a way to solve a common writer's problem.

- Respond to content FIRST.

- Celebrate small victories (because it takes a lifetime to become a writer).

DON'T ...

- Assess everything.
- Correct everything students write.
- Do students' editing for them.
- Let worksheets replace writing time.
- Be afraid to share your writing with students. You can do it. **DO** it.
- Worry too much about conventional correctness—yet!
- Demand revision/editing—<u>model</u> it, though.
- Forget to read aloud, often, with expression & joy.
- Overlook the tiny details, the little moments of voice, the new conventions, the special words that show your writers are growing, learning.
- Forget to point these strengths out to your writers who have a bigger need to know than you, than parents, than the district, than <u>anyone</u>. They **NEED** to know.
- Let any excuse in the world keep you from being a writer yourself.
- Forget to let students see how much you love books, writing, & teaching.

Chapter 6

TEACHING TRAITS TO PRIMARY WRITERS

GOALS FOR PRIMARY WRITERS

- **To experience joy in writing**
- **To love the sound of words**
- **To want to write often**
- **To create for others & for yourself**
- **To become an audience for the writing of others**
- **To love literature & love being a listener**
- **To discover new & favorite books, authors**
- **To try writing in many forms ...**
  - ✎ **Pictures**
  - ✎ **Dictation**
  - ✎ **Story boarding**
  - ✎ **Text**
- **To aim for READABLE spelling that helps your reader**
- **To write for more than one audience**
- **To look around ... & <u>see</u>, notice, & borrow**

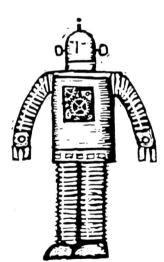

Adapted from Spandel and Stiggins, <u>Creating Writers</u>, 1997.

GOALS FOR PRIMARY TEACHERS

- To celebrate students' love of writing
- To see not what is <u>missing</u> ... but what is <u>there</u>
- To teach ourselves to identify moments of voice, details, expressiveness, exploration with conventions
- To help students recognize & build on their strengths
- To respond to content first
- To respond to the writer, not the writing
- To control the anxiety that urges us toward too much perfection too soon
- To see exploration as an achievement
- To help students see that writing is thinking, & conventions exist to serve ideas
- To give students the language they need to think like writers
- To share with expression, passion, voice & heart the books WE love
- To write ... & to share with students the adventures of our writing
- To nurture within ourselves a bedrock belief in the power of children to do amazing things

SIX IMPORTANT TIPS

1. DON'T WORRY ABOUT NUMBERS.

The key to good assessment at this level is watching for signs of development. Describe what you see—but don't worry about putting a number on it. Language tells more than numbers. Consider using a developmental continuum as a checklist to document growth and keep a running record of expanding skills. The time to begin using numbers is when students themselves can begin to interpret what those numbers mean.

2. HELP STUDENTS DEVELOP A WRITER'S VOCABULARY.

Use every opportunity you can to refer to "clear ideas," "strong feelings" (voice), "an interesting way to begin [or end]" (organization), "words that help you picture things in your mind," etc. Use the language of the traits to talk about books or other writings you share aloud, to respond to students' own work, and to talk about your own writing. Help your students begin to think like writers. Give them a working vocabulary for talking to each other and to you about their writing.

3. SEE WHAT IS THERE, NOT WHAT'S MISSING.

Look for what's <u>there</u>, not what's missing. You cannot appreciate too deeply. You cannot enjoy too much. Every writer wants his or her work valued. Learn to see the real growth that lies within each child's efforts, see the intelligence behind the "errors," and your responses will be both genuine and encouraging. Do not fret over what isn't happening yet. It will come when the time is right. So-called "mistakes" are often the beginnings of development.

4. READ, READ, & READ SOME MORE!

Use the language all around you as a way of discussing what works and doesn't work in writing. Talk about the books you read aloud. What do you—or your students—like? What don't you like? Why? Link your comments to the traits.... "Did you ever notice how some books have the power to make you want to keep reading? You just can't stop? There's a word for that kind of power—it's called VOICE." Use poetry, too, letters from friends, articles from the newspaper, directions you get with your new blender, a set of written directions to a place you've never been (could you really find it?), descriptions of shows in <u>TV Guide</u>, recipes, menus, pamphlets from the veterinarian or dentist's office. Bits and pieces from everywhere. Some good, some not so good. Read them and talk about them so that students begin to notice some writing is a lot better than other writing.

> *R*eading aloud is not a cure-all. Not quite.
> But it is such a wonderful antidote for turning on turned-off readers and brightening up dull writing that I feel it's worthwhile to plead again for its regular occurrence in every classroom . . .That is why I'm closing these particular remarks in an attitude of supplication, begging for teachers to read aloud, once more, with feeling, every day of their classroom lives.
>
> *Mem Fox*
> *Radical Reflections, 70*

5. MODEL REVISION, BUT DON'T DEMAND IT.

When you're working on a story or essay of your own, read it aloud to your class. Talk about your plans for revision. You might say, "I'm not happy with the ideas yet. I think I need to say more about why I was so frightened of the dog. I don't think a reader can tell that from my story, do you?" That's enough. Just suggest gently that revising is something writers do. Be sure to share the revised version, too—but don't imply you've "fixed it." Students need to understand that revision is "seeing it again," bringing it into focus, zeroing in on the details a quick glance misses, or sometimes, expanding the original idea because you just think of more details the next time around, or you think of something else your audience/reader will need or want to know. Revision is not for the incompetent. On the contrary,

REVISION IS FOR THINKERS !

6. TAKE A BROAD VIEW OF WRITING.

Scribbles are imitative, and show that students recognize the importance and value of writing. Pictures are valid forms of communication (and become extraordinarily sophisticated in the hands of writers/artists who continue to use them). Primary students learn to be writers by being listeners first, hearing and responding to stories and to many other kinds of text as well. Acknowledge their ability to listen critically, and to share back what, specifically, has moved them or given their imagination a little nudge.

> As teachers, we place great emphasis on letters and words as we eagerly await the emergence of the young writer. In doing so, we often overlook the value of drawing as a composing process. We need to look more closely, to ask questions, to listen—even if there are yet no words to the story.
>
> *Kathy Matthews*
> "A Child Composes," in *Understanding Writing*, 13

Let them put their thinking skills to work in planning writing with you. Planning is a form of writing, too, even when you're the only one holding the pencil! Write letters, memos, reminder lists, thank you notes. Engage them in the design process. Discuss content. Choose words together. Talk about length, beginnings, endings, questions your audience will have. Illustrate some things you write together (a great way to build skills in both ideas and organization!).

TEACHING TRAITS TO PRIMARY WRITERS
QUICK SUMMARY

1. Don't worry about numbers

- Describe the strengths you see

2. Help students develop a writer's vocabulary

- Comment on their work
- Ask them to comment on what you read aloud

3. Look for what they're doing well—not mistakes

- Details
- New discoveries in conventions
- Self-expression (voice)

4. Read—as often as you can!

Help students ...

- hear the voice
- listen for details (ideas)
- draw pictures of what they "see" (ideas)
- make predictions (organization)
- listen for the rhythm & flow (fluency)
- identify favorite words (word choice)

5. Model more than you demand

- Prewriting & planning
- Drafting
- Revision & reflection
- Sharing

6. Let writing take many forms

- Pictures—illustrate a picture book
- Dictation
- Oral storytelling
- Planning—for you or older student writers
- Labeling (models, charts, maps)
- Text

WHERE'S THE CONNECTION TO THE TRAITS?

You may be wondering what you will need to do differently to teach the traits to your students. Assuming you are allowing time for writing, and encouraging your students to write often, remarkably little!

In fact, you may be surprised how much many of the writing activities you are using right now support the traits. Try this: Think of a writing activity you have found successful. Meaning that your students enjoyed it, were engaged and involved, and also learned something important about writing.

Here's one example: In a K-1 class recently, we read a book by Jack Gantos called <u>Rotten Ralph</u>. The students loved the book, and I asked them to tell me why. Here were their responses:

- It was funny!
- The pictures made me laugh.
- My cat is rude like Ralph.
- I like cats. I like books about cats.
- The writing is expressive.

I was especially intrigued by the last comment, so I asked the student if she knew another word for "expressive."

"Why, yes," she told me without hesitation. "It has voice."

That is the goal in a nutshell—student writers with the language and the vocabulary to think and speak like writers.

We then talked about writing to Jack Gantos to tell him how much we had enjoyed the book. These young writers were not yet composing text as long as a paragraph, so I offered to be their stenographer if they would dictate their letter to me. With happy eyes and many smiles, they agreed. There were 13 students in the group, so we had to take turns, but they were exceptionally good at this, and here is the letter we wrote together:

Dear Mr. Gantos:

We really loved your book about Rotten Ralph. It was funny. It was really funny. Ralph is so werd (sic). We really loved the book. We love to write. We would like to know where you get your ideas.

Sincerely,

Mrs. Moore's Transitional Class

Which traits were we focusing on in this lesson? All of them, really. Here's how:

IDEAS

As writers compose, they must think constantly of content—what to include, and how to support it through elaboration or detail. These young writers did their own thinking. That's the hardest part of writing. Even though I actually put the words on the paper, they put the ideas together.

ORGANIZATION

Every piece of writing requires the writer to ask him- or herself, "How should I begin? What should I say next? How should I end it?" I prompted the students with these very questions to encourage them to think about their beginning, how to connect ideas, how to end a letter gracefully.

VOICE

Letter writing is one of the best ways I know to teach voice. When students write letters, they have a definite audience in mind. Sometimes, it's helpful to put a face with the audience. You can do this. Bring in a poster with a favorite author, sports figure, celebrity, news journalist, or any famous person your students will recognize.

Ask them to write to that person, and notice the difference in voice. In this case, we were writing to someone who had just spoken to us through his work. It felt as natural as talking on the phone. That's how friendly, informal writing should feel.

WORD CHOICE

These writers were stuck on the idea of <u>Rotten Ralph</u> being funny (which it is). But I wanted them to explore a little. "Tell me something else," I said.

"He's weird," they said. Great! We added that.

SENTENCE FLUENCY

Composing in sentences seems to come naturally even to very young students composing letters. I did ask them to tell me where each sentence ended, and they had no trouble with this.

CONVENTIONS

What a natural for dictation! We stopped frequently to talk about what we were doing and why, and I let them make <u>all</u> the decisions about punctuation and capitalization. I asked them questions like these:

- How should we begin? (*"Dear Mr. Gantos ..."*)
- Should I call him "Jack" or "Mr. Gantos"? *(Mr. Gantos)*
- What comes after the "Mr"? *(A period)*
- What comes after "Gantos"? *(A period, they told me. We put it in, then later changed it to a comma after checking to see what other writers do.)*
- Do I have to capitalize "Gantos"? Why?
- Does this letter need to be capitalized? *(First letter of the sentence. Yes.)*
- How should I end my sentence? *(With a period)*
- How do you know I need a period here? *(End of sentence)*
- Should I use a question mark instead? *(No way!)*
- Why?
- How should we close our letter? *(Sincerely)*
- What comes after "Sincerely"? *(They disagreed. Some thought a comma, some a period, one wanted a colon. We looked at a sample letter my secretary had sent to one of the children in the class to see what she had done.)*

When we got to the word "weird," I told them I was stuck and needed their help to sound it out. They leaped to the task, and used all their phonetic skills to advise me. They had clearly done this before, and their guess was skillful, and close. I used their suggestion. We could have followed this up by looking in the dictionary or looking on a spell checker to help us, but the main point was made: If you aren't sure, get help, work together, problem solve, figure it out.

A WORD ABOUT "WRITING"

To someone visiting Mrs. Moore's class that afternoon, it might have looked as if I was the one doing all the writing. After all, I was the one holding the pen and the tablet. Actually, however, I was only recording (and to some extent, coaching) the real writing that was occurring. Writing is about 90 percent planning, thinking, problem solving, deciding, trying, revising, and asking yourself questions. The primary years are a perfect time to involve beginning writers in this kind of decisionmaking. That way, when they have the motor coordination that enables them to generate their own text with some ease, they will have in place the thinking to support that physical part of the writing process. And then much of the battle will have been won.

YOUR TURN

Now it's your turn. Think of one or two writing activities you have enjoyed and felt good about using with your students. Then ask yourself, what skills did my students need to do those activities? What questions were they posing to themselves? What writer's problems were they solving? Think beyond the physical act of writing. Remember, if your students are sorting and grouping, they are building organizational skills. If they are noticing details about a pet hamster you keep in your classroom, you are helping them become careful, thoughtful observers; that's the foundation for idea development. Writing is BIG. So, please, think expansively. Don't just picture your students with pencils in their hands. Picture them thinking like writers. To help you make the connection, check out the short lists of questions under each trait on the following pages.

HOW TO IDENTIFY THE TRAITS IN YOUR CLASSROOM ACTIVITIES

1. DOES THIS ACTIVITY ENCOURAGE ...

- Observing details? Noticing things? Paying attention?
- Making pictures—in your mind? Or on paper?
- Listening for what is interesting?
- Listening for what is unusual?
- Drawing inferences (Whose shoe might this be?)?

If so, you are reinforcing **IDEAS.**

2. DOES THIS ACTIVITY ENCOURAGE ...

- Putting things in order?
- Grouping like things together (by color, shape, size, etc.)?
- Making predictions (What will happen next? How will it end?)?
- Deciding how to begin?
- Deciding how to end (e.g., Help me end this note to my friend.)?
- Recalling events in a story?

If so, you are reinforcing **ORGANIZATION.**

3. DOES THIS ACTIVITY ENCOURAGE ...

- Individual responses (responses which are unique for each child)?
- Expression of both ideas & feelings?
- Thinking about your feelings?
- Listening to & talking about literature with lots of voice?
- Expressing opinions?
- Learning to recognize writers' unique voices?
- Writing to an audience?

If so, you are reinforcing VOICE.

4. DOES THIS ACTIVITY ENCOURAGE ...

- Listening for or learning new words?
- Saying something more than one way?
- Thinking about the meaning of words?
- Identifying favorite words?
- Listening to language used well?
- Learning about resources (dictionary, thesaurus, etc.)?
- Playing with words?

If so, you are reinforcing WORD CHOICE.

5. DOES THIS ACTIVITY ENCOURAGE ...

- Thinking about what a sentence is?
- Listening to literature that has rhythm?
- Reading aloud? Choral reading?
- Comparing two kinds of sentences (choppy vs. fluid)?
- Comparing sentences to fragments?
- Combining sentences?

If so, you are reinforcing **SENTENCE FLUENCY**.

6. DOES THIS ACTIVITY ENCOURAGE ...

- Noticing the print all around us?
- Thinking about & talking about the **MEANING** behind the conventions?
- Looking & talking about examples of conventions used well?
- Exploring the use of new conventions?
- Learning labels (What is a margin? What is a comma? Can you find one?)?
- Learning & using copy editor's symbols?
- Connecting sounds to letters?
- Thinking like an editor (Name on paper? Spaces between words?)?

If so, you are reinforcing **CONVENTIONS**.

ReMeMBeR ...

✎ There are many possibilities not listed here!! This list is just to help you make connections between your successful activities & the traits you are reinforcing through those activities.

✎ A single activity can connect to more than one trait. It may reinforce two, three—or all six! Great.

CLASSROOM ACTIVITIES FOR TEACHING TRAITS TO BEGINNING WRITERS

Let's begin by acknowledging that the single most important thing to "build" in primary writers is a sense of joy in writing. Nothing replaces that. At the same time, success builds confidence—and confidence feels good. So in a very real way,

Success equals Joy.

Further, you don't have to do <u>these very activities</u> to build students' skills. Far from it. These are just guidelines to get you started. Please add your own successful activities to this list—and keep it growing!

TEACHING
IDEAS

WHAT YOU'RE GOING FOR

🖉 Awareness of details

🖉 Ability to see what others miss

🖉 Knowing what's most important or interesting

🖉 A good sense of the "main point" or "main storyline"

SUGGESTED ACTIVITIES

1. BE OBSERVERS

Ask students to be observers of their surroundings. See how much they notice. Record their observations. You can do this on a nature hike, for instance, or by observing a classroom pet, such as a chameleon, hamster, rabbit, or fish. Don't stop too soon, either. Make them dig a little. Keep them working on it till they really cannot come up with more. Then say, 'OK, of all the things we noticed, which are most interesting? Most important? Most unusual? Which details would you like to read about?"

2. USE PICTURES

to draw out summary lists of details. Greeting cards and postcards are good sources for unusual, colorful, and interesting pictures. Collect them. If students are old enough to write their own lists, let them work in groups. A more advanced version of this is to have students describe a picture, then see if others can recognize it from the description.

3. WRITE A SHORT PIECE

yourself about a friend, pet, experience, etc. Before you write, invite students to make a list of questions they would like to ask and have you answer in the paper. Record all their questions, then read them back. Then tell students, "I will <u>only answer five</u> of your questions in my writing, so choose <u>carefully</u>." Let them talk in groups or pairs for a couple minutes to choose favorites, then make a class list. If they cannot agree, you might try writing two different paragraphs, answering two different sets of questions, then talk about the differences. Which one is better? Which holds your interest more? Why?

4. ASK FOR QUESTIONS

As you share longer written pieces orally, ask, "What questions do you hope this writer will answer? What do you want him (or her) to tell next?"

5. DRAW WHAT YOU SEE & FEEL

Ask students to draw as they listen to literature. Draw what they feel and what they see. Then give them time to share: What did you <u>feel</u>? What did you <u>see in your mind</u>? Why do you think you saw it that way?

6. OOPS! WHERE DID THE DETAILS GO?

Rewrite a story that's familiar to your students, but take out all the details and juicy tidbits you can. Share the story, e.g., "Once upon a time there were three pigs. Two were not very good builders. One was pretty good. The pigs that were not good builders got eaten by a wolf. The pig that was a good builder got away." Ask what's missing. Share the original story and ask what makes it better.

7. CREATE A GROUP PICTURE

of a busy scene; e.g., shopping mall, zoo, grocery store, carnival, fair, city street, crowded beach, etc. Allow everyone to add details—call them details. At the end, talk about how many things you've thought of, how some people remembered things others had forgotten, etc. If possible, let this project span several days or more so that students have time to think, reflect, remember. Talk about how you don't necessarily remember everything right away, but things sift into your mind little by little.

TEACHING

ORGANIZATION

WHAT YOU'RE GOING FOR

✐ Sense of sequence

✐ Ability to organize & group

✐ Sense of beginning

✐ Sense of ending

SUGGESTED ACTIVITIES

1. WAS THIS A GOOD LEAD?

When you read stories (or other literature or writings) aloud, pause after the beginning to ask, "Why do you think the writer started this way?" Alternative: BEFORE beginning, ask, "Where do you think the writer will begin?"

2. PREDICT!

As you are reading, ask, "What do you think will happen next? What will this writer talk about next? How do you think it might end?"

3. LISTEN FOR THE END

Read a short story aloud and ask students to listen for the ending. Ask them to raise their hands when they think you have come to the end of the story. (Be careful to pick one without a too-obvious "lived happily ever after" sort of ending.)

4. USE STORY BOARDING

Tell stories with pictures using two, three, four or more story board blocks to convey different events. Variation: Give pairs or groups of three a story board sequence in pictures. Have them put the pictures in order showing what happens first, next, next, last. Ask them to talk about the clues they used in deciding on the "right" order. Could there be more than one order?

5. USE GROUPING

Give students lots of opportunities to group things together that go together: colors, shapes, sizes. Any category will do.

6. GIVE ME SOME TIPS!

Ask for students' help in organizing a paper of your own. Say you are writing a paper on black bears. Put two, three, or four major categories on the board: How they look, what they eat, how they act around people, etc. Use any categories you think are appropriate. Then, one by one, list for students the bits of information you want to put in your paper. You should have a dozen or so tidbits of information. Ask them to tell you which category is most appropriate.

7. WAS THAT THE END??!!

As you're reading, omit the ending from a piece. Ask students to make up their own to either write or share orally.

8. CAN YOU PUT THESE IN ORDER?

For readers, list three or four events that occur in a story. Ask them to put these in order. Next step: Expand the list to include one or two events that really don't belong. Ask students, "What could you leave out? Is there something that might go better in another story?"

9. WHAT DOESN'T BELONG?

As you read a short piece, insert a comment or sentence that clearly does not belong. Ask students to identify it by writing it out, or just by raising their hands. Can they explain why it did not fit?

TEACHING VOICE

WHAT YOU'RE GOING FOR

🖉 Feelings

🖉 Enthusiasm for writing

🖉 Individuality

🖉 Passion

SUGGESTED ACTIVITIES

1. READ! READ! READ!

Read and discuss lots of literature with voice. Look everywhere. Picture books are great (see <u>Picture Books: An Annotated Bibliography,</u> described in the chapter on "Using Reading to Teach Writing," for more ideas); but they're not the only source. Also check the paper, and magazines (especially ads, movie reviews, book reviews, and editorials). Check food labels, brochures, junk mail, etc. Go for the strong <u>and</u> the weak, always asking, "Did you like this writing? Would you like to hear more? Why? Why not?" Join in these discussions yourself. Let it be known that you value and seek voice in writing. If you run across something you love in your own reading, bring it in to share—even if it's difficult. Your love of good language and feeling is more important to convey than the meaning of the text.

2. LOOK FOR INDIVIDUALITY

in both pictures and print. Point it out. Praise students for their differences: "This is so unusual, so unlike anyone else's!"

3. PLAY THE "VOICE" GAME

Students can sit at their desks for this, but it works much better if they gather in a circle on the floor or outside on the lawn, where seating is random. Ask students to close their eyes as you roam through the group. Periodically, touch a student gently on the head or shoulder; that's their signal to say, "Hello out there" (or any phrase of your choice). Others try to guess who is speaking. After the game, talk about how you recognize different voices.

4. WHO WROTE THIS?

Ask students to complete a thought or share opinions on the same topic. For example, you might ask everyone, "The BEST thing (or WORST thing) about school is ... ." Keep responses private. Share them later individually and anonymously to see if classmates can recognize one another's responses. (Let students know in advance you will be playing this guessing game.)

5. WHAT IS THE WRITER LIKE?

As you share literature, ask students, "What kind of person is the writer? What do you picture? If you had lunch with this person, what would he/she be like?"

6. SHARE TWO VERY DIFFERENT PIECES OF WRITING

by different authors. Ask students which piece they think has more voice. Then, share a third piece by one of the authors—a piece that has the same sound as the first one by the same author. Ask students to identify the writer of the third piece. Ask them to explain how they knew which one it was.

7. BE ON THE LOOKOUT!

Search for posters, postcards, greeting cards, etc., that convey voice through originality, unusual perspective, color, sensitivity, humor, or general "personality." Ask students what they see in the art or photography that they like. "Does it look like anyone else's? Is that good? Why?"

8. USE METAPHOR

Which **FOODS** have a lot of voice? Which **COLORS** have the most voice? Suppose you dressed yourself in **CLOTHES** with lots of voice; what might your outfit look like?

9. HELP THE PROS REVISE

Take a simple piece of writing, such as a greeting card, and ask students for suggestions on revising it to add voice: e.g., "Thanks for the good time." What could you say that would have a little more punch, pizzazz, personality?

10. WRITE NOTES & LETTERS

Nothing brings out voice like writing to a real audience. Have students work with you to compose a simple original piece with lots of voice—preferably a "real" piece of writing to which you might expect a response. Example: A note of thanks to someone who visits the classroom; OR, a business note written to a local business to express appreciation or even a complaint; OR, a letter to a writer whose work you particularly admire. Be sure to share the reason behind the note before you and your students begin thinking through how to compose. Share the response too, if you get one.

TEACHING

WORD CHOICE

WHAT YOU'RE GOING FOR

✏ Awareness of language

✏ Awareness that there are different ways to say things

✏ Love of favorite words

SUGGESTED ACTIVITIES

1. COLLECT FAVORITE WORDS

Make lists. Decorate them on colored paper and post them or hang them from the ceilings. Make mobiles. Make word collages. Encourage labeling—but be creative. Put adjectives with the nouns: e.g., not just "wall," but "drab green wall" perhaps.

2. RETIRE TIRED WORDS

Put the words you're tired of in a shoe box and bury them.

3. BRAINSTORM ALTERNATIVES

to the tired words in item #2. Put them on word wheels: these are shaped like daisies, with the tired word at the center and creative options on petals rotating out from the center. Mount word wheels on walls or ceilings.

4. LISTEN!

As you share literature (or any writing!), ask students to listen for a favorite word or two. Share with a partner or the whole class. Or write them in a journal (for writer-readers). Or, <u>you</u> write three or four or more on the board. Guess how to spell as you go for younger reader-writers.

5. BRAINSTORM ALTERNATIVES

Suppose you are writing a note to a friend. It might begin like this: "I had a good time at your house." Tell your students, "I'm tired of the word *good*. Help me out. What else could I say? What are some other ways to say this?" Do this often, so that looking for alternatives begins to feel natural.

6. GUESSING IS THINKING

Sometimes you can make a good guess about the meaning of a word using topic or context as clues (also, pictures in picture books). Help students find thoughtful, imaginative ways to guess at meanings of words that are new. Brainstorm several alternatives before giving them the answer. Encourage guessing. Encourage thinking.

7. GET A WORD-A-DAY CALENDAR

for kids, and let them guess what today's word might mean. Alternative: Play the word meaning game. Give the real definition to one child. Two other volunteers make up their own definitions for the new word. All three share their definitions orally with the class; students try to guess which one is accurate. This only takes about five minutes per word, so you can play two or three rounds. Great for vocabulary and imagination. (Yes, they **DO** remember the correct definition!)

8. PUT GOOD RESOURCES TO WORK—OFTEN!

Let students see you frequently using word meaning resources—such as a good dictionary of synonyms. Allow one student to choose a word they would like to hear synonyms for. Look it up and share the synonyms orally.

9. IS THIS APPROPRIATE?

Write two very different versions of one note—say a complaint about school lunches you might write to the principal of your school and another note on the same topic you might write to a friend in another city. See if students can tell from the language you use which note goes where. Ask them to explain how they know. Were there particular words or phrases that gave it away?

TEACHING
SENTENCE FLUENCY

WHAT YOU'RE GOING FOR

🖋 An ear for language

🖋 A love of rhythm

🖋 Sentence sense

SUGGESTED ACTIVITIES

1. SHARE RHYTHMIC LANGUAGE

that's fun to read aloud. Poetry is an excellent choice, but be sure the rhymes are creative and the language natural. Some poems work so hard at rhyming that much of the natural flow is lost. Rehearse. Read it aloud before you share it with students, so it will feel natural. Remember that some prose pieces have wonderful rhythm, too. Hearing good language read aloud builds fluency <u>even in young writers who are themselves not yet ready to begin writing sentences.</u>

2. SHARE TWO VERSIONS

of writing with the same content but a very different sound. Write one with short, choppy sentences: *We went to the beach. It was sunny. It was warm. We had fun. We flew kites. We ate snacks.* VERSUS: *We spent a warm, sunny day at the beach eating snacks and flying kites.* Ask students which they prefer and why. You may need to share a number of examples before students begin to hear the differences. Don't give up. Keep sharing. Keep asking.

3. PLAY THE SENTENCE BUILDING GAME

You can do this on the board or just orally. Have students choose a topic: money, baseball, school, cats, etc. Then, you come up with sentence beginnings, and ask them to finish each sentence. Give them only one sentence beginning at a time. The only rule is you have to make a complete sentence. For instance, you might come up with the beginning "In the morning ... ." When students add their ending, the sentence might turn into "In the morning OUR CAT IS HUNGRY." The purpose of the game is to help students become aware that sentences can begin in many ways. So use your imagination to come up with lots of variety. Use six or seven beginnings or more each time you play. Variation: Let them give YOU the beginnings, and you come up with the answers by completing the sentences.

144

4. IS IT A SENTENCE OR FRAGMENT?

Play this like a spelling bee, with teams lined up. One side plays first, then the other. To remain standing, students must give the right answer. You give the questions: Ask each student, "Is this a sentence or fragment?" Then give an example: *My cousin Mary, Come inside, Where is your umbrella? The ugly old baboon,* etc. The idea is for students to develop an ear for sentences and to learn to hear the difference between sentences and fragments. Make the examples <u>very easy</u> at first, then gradually harder as students get better at the game. The team with the most people left standing at the end wins.

TEACHING
CONVENTIONS

WHAT YOU'RE GOING FOR

✎ Awareness of writing conventions

✎ Willingness to experiment

✎ Patience to take a second look

SUGGESTED ACTIVITIES

1. BEGIN SIMPLY

Assign editing tasks that are appropriate for age and ability. A good first editing activity is to check for your name on your paper. Is it there? Be sure you refer to this as <u>editing</u>, and reward students for having the patience to go back and check for this detail. Gradually, add other simple things as appropriate: e.g., a title on the paper or picture, a date on the piece. Eventually, beginning writers can also add such things as space between words, vertical space between lines, left-to-right orientation on the page, etc.

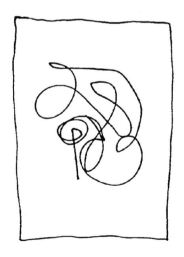 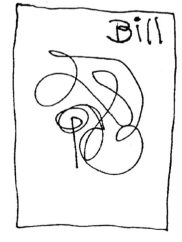

146

2. ENCOURAGE YOUNG WRITERS TO THINK LIKE EDITORS

As students begin to generate their own conventional text (multiple words, beginning sentences, punctuated phrases and sentences), routinely and frequently ask WHY: Why did you put a period here? Why did you put a capital letter here? This helps reinforce the thinking behind the conventions.

3. CELEBRATE DISCOVERIES

without worrying overmuch about correctness: e.g., "Robert—I see you've discovered periods! You have lots of them in your writing now."

4. ENCOURAGE EXPERIMENTATION

Reward students for trying something new. For noticing. For attempting to copy. For asking questions. Exploration is an end in itself; when it stops, learning stops with it. We do NOT need to assess everything, nor is it useful to do so while students are in their exploring/experimenting phase. If we expect and look for correct text all the time, we'll get precious little of it.

5. SEE WHAT IS THERE

not what is missing. Make sure students also <u>know</u> what they are doing well. Left-right orientation? Spaces between words? Using letters to indicate sounds? Readable spelling, or pretty close? Applaud little victories. Point them out to students and DO NOT WORRY YET ABOUT "ERRORS," which are only the young writers' imagination at work.

6. TEACH COPY EDITOR'S MARKS

just as soon as your young editors are ready. This usually means as soon as they begin to write in sentences or near-sentences. <u>A list of symbols appropriate for and useful to primary writers</u> appears in the section on "Beginning Editing," immediately following this section.

7. HELP STUDENTS DEVELOP A PROOFREADER'S EYE!

Once students are beginning to write conventional text, and once they are familiar with copy editors' symbols, give them editing practice on **TEXT THAT IS NOT THEIR OWN. This is critical. Editing their own work is the MOST DIFFICULT editing task we could give them. Build skills first by allowing them to spot and correct errors in the work of <u>others</u>** (any editor will tell you how much easier this is).

Beware, however: Do <u>not</u> ask students to edit the text of other students—this is touchy business, and besides, it's too hard to control the practice, and MUCH, MUCH too hard for students to edit other students' work. The text is often unclear and difficult to read. Further, students often give each other editing advice that is <u>incorrect</u>. This makes the teaching of editing very difficult (not to mention making the student editors, and you, cranky). <u>For editing practice, ALWAYS use text from a book or invent your own.</u>

Keep the practice <u>very short</u> and do not include many mistakes at first. As with the scavenger hunt, make it a searching game—this time with students looking for what's wrong. A beginning editor's text might look like this:

The cat at two mise

There are three mistakes in the "two mise" sentence. Some students may find all three. Some may find just the missing period—or just the missing "e" from "ate." That's great—it's a beginning. Do not grade these exercises. Just play the game regularly, always asking, "How many errors are in this text? What are they?" Let students work with partners. Give them plenty of time. Keep the task simple. Once students know proofreader's marks, their final edited copy will look

The cat at two mise

The cat at two mise

7. HOST A PUNCTUATION SCAVENGER HUNT

Print out a SHORT paragraph of text and make enough copies so you can give one to every two students. Make sure the copy is LARGE and easy to read, with BIG spaces between words and BIG spaces vertically, too. Also make sure there are many different marks of punctuation used. Then, identify a mark (e.g., *a period)* and see which team can find an example first. Let the first finders help the others locate the mark you're looking for. Then ask if anyone knows why it is there. Even non-readers and beginning readers can play this game if you keep it simple enough. They can begin to identify periods and question marks.

Variation #1: See if students can identify key words: e.g., "Who can find the word DOG in your paragraph? Put your finger on it when you find it." Gradually, add more skills, more difficult questions: e.g., "Who can find the longest sentence? Who can find a semicolon? Who can find quotation marks? Who can find a name of a person?" You decide what questions are appropriate.

Variation #2: Let students who identify an item correctly ask the next question.

8. LET STUDENT EDITORS BE THE AUTHORITIES

Ask, "How can I show ... ?" You want to write a question, let's say:

What time is it

Say to students, "How can I show that this is a question? How will my reader know?" Let students "problem solve" with you to find the right punctuation mark for the situation:

What time is it ?

As students gain skills, ask for help with longer pieces, <u>looking for the same things you ask them to look for.</u> Put a piece on the overhead, for instance, that has no title. Ask them to tell you what's missing—then let them help you brainstorm a good title! Keep the editing tasks simple, short, and manageable.

9. GROUP SPELLING

Gather students in a group. Let four or five students choose any word they'd like to spell. Ask students to hear the word in their heads first, then try to picture it as you pronounce it slowly and carefully. Then, work together sounding it out as you write it on the board. Take SWAMP, for instance. You might say, "OK, what sound do you hear first? How do you think it starts? S-S-S- That's an S—let's put that on the board.... What sound do you hear next?" and so on. Students have the fun of playing with words, but they're learning word sounds—on words of their choosing.

10. INVENTIVE SPELLING

As students begin to write, encourage inventive spelling and punctuating, but explain WHY. This is important. Students—like many parents—may be reluctant to accept this way of doing things if they think it will lead to poor work, mistakes, and low grades. Help them understand that making a best guess is NOT the same as being careless. Rather, it's a way of <u>building</u> skills by connecting letters to sounds. Eventually, this skill will be supplemented by

- memorization of key sight words
- use of a dictionary
- use of a speller's handbook
- use of a computer spell checker
- increased proofreader's skills
- assistance from a qualified editor

Like early attempts to walk, talk and draw,
initial attempts to spell do not produce habits to be overcome. No one worries when a child's first drawing of a person is a head propped up on two stick legs. As the errors become more sophisticated—two stick arms protruding from the head where the ears should be—no one fears this schema will become a habit, though it may be repeated a hundred times … . [These errors] are greeted as a display of intelligence and emerging proficiency."

Susan Sowers

"Six Questions Teachers Ask About Invented Spelling," *Understanding Writing*, 62

11. EXPLAIN WHEN & WHY EDITING IS IMPORTANT

You may wish to distinguish between "book language" and "first draft language." Does everything need to be in "book language"? How about the grocery list? A phone message? A note to a buddy? A note to your mom? A poem? A birthday greeting? A report on eagles? A memo written by someone in the school office? A letter your mom writes to the school principal? A letter you write to the president? How do you decide when correctness really COUNTS? What is the role of the editor? When do we need to call in an editor to help us with our work? Why do even professional writers use editors? Talking this through makes these decisions more comfortable. Don't be surprised to discover you need to talk this over <u>quite a lot</u>.

12. HEY! I FOUND A MISTAKE HERE!

Give experienced student editors a chance to look for mistakes in <u>real printed text</u>—not just text you create for editing practice. If you discover a mistake in newspaper headline, for instance, put it on an overhead and see if they can spot it too.

13. LET STUDENTS BE THEIR OWN EDITORS

This is vital. Edit for students **ONLY** when

- the piece is going to be formally published somewhere

- the student writer has gone as far with the editing herself as her skills will permit

- the writer approves/requests/sanctions your intervention

BeGiNNiNG EdiTiNG

In teaching editing to very young writers, think of the general purpose for editing:

To take a last look and be sure everything is in order.

Give young writers tasks they can manage themselves in taking this last look; this allows them to be responsible for their own editing. At primary levels, don't worry about conventionally correct spelling and punctuation unless the piece is to be formally published and the child wants it in correct book form. Then if the child cannot handle all the editing, you can say, appropriately, "This is the time for some help from another editor. You have a copy of your work in **KIDS' WRITING**. Let's also make a copy in **BOOK WRITING** so that everyone can read it, and when you get older, you can still read it too." This gives value and respect to what the child has done, and also introduces her to the world of formal publishing, in which **ALL** authors (not just the struggling ones, thank goodness!) have ready access to an editor's help. That other editor might be you, an older student, or a parent volunteer.

Here are some things <u>very</u> young editors can be responsible for:

- ♣ **Name on paper**
- ♣ **Title**
- ♣ **Margins**
- ♣ **Spaces between words**
- ♣ **left**
- ♣ **Any words out**

THOUGHTS ON PRIMARY EDITING

1. Not every piece needs to be perfect. Do NOT spend precious writing time editing <u>everything</u> your students write. What is the point? <u>Your</u> editing skills will soar, but what they learn is minimal! Remember, our goal is not to fill the world with perfect pieces of writing, but to fill the world with skillful writers and editors. There is only one way to make this happen ...

Students must do their own editing.

2. Let them practice editing—often. Keep the practice simple and short. Focus on one or two errors at a time. Ask, "What's missing from this sentence?" OR, "What did I forget?" OR, "How would you edit this?" Then, on the chalk board or overhead, share a sample like one of these:

- **Bob is here**

- **bob is here.**

- **Is Bob here**

- **Is Bob heer?**

Gradually, make the task a little harder (two or three errors or two kinds of errors), taking your cue from what students can handle readily. If YOU have to do it for them, it is too hard. If they can do it, it's just right. Go to the next step. Practice every day. Call it <u>editing</u>.

COPY EDITOR'S SYMBOLS
PRIMARY & EARLY ELEMENTARY

Symbol	Meaning	Example
⟍	Take it out.	I'm a good ~~good~~ singer.
∧	Put something in.	*good* I'm a ∧ singer.
⌗	Put in space.	I'm agood singer. ∧⌗
⊙	Add a period.	I'm a good singer⊙
≡	Make this letter a capital.	i'm a good singer. ≡
╱	Make this capital lower case.	I'm a Good singer.
SP	Spelling error	I'm a good (sinnger).

3. **Use copy editor's symbols. It's professional, and it teaches students to think like writers/editors.**

4. **Use editing language. Call conventions by that name—"conventions."**

5. **Ask students to think about why we edit. What would happen if everyone spelled things differently? If everyone used different punctuation symbols? What if we made up our own? Let them try it for a day!**

6. **Use environmental print as much as possible. Ask,**

   - **Why do you think the writer used a capital letter here?**
   - **What does this mark (pointing to a punctuation mark) mean?**
   - **This print is bigger. Why do you think the writer did that?**
   - **This writer put a picture here. Was that a good idea?**
   - **Writers often use titles. Why? Do they help?**

7. **Let writers practice on the writing of others. Do NOT ask them to edit their own work every time. This is tedious, and will encourage many young writers not to write much (it's like building a tiny house so you won't have so much to dust).**

8. **Let writers keep a working file, and occasionally choose a piece of their own they would like to edit, illustrate, or otherwise prepare for publication.**

9. **Occasionally, encourage writers to work in teams to write, edit, and illustrate. After all, this is how it works in real life. Rarely does one person do even two of these tasks, let alone all three. Use credits from picture books to show students that in most cases, one person writes, one illustrates, and another edits.**

As a society, we allow children to learn to speak by trial and error. But when it comes to reading and writing, we expect them to be right the first time.

Donald Graves and Virginia Stuart

Write From the Start, 34

EDITING PRACTICE
FIVE SAMPLE MINI-LESSONS

TIPS

1. Practice daily. Most student editors get very infrequent practice with their editing skills. It is next to impossible to develop a proofreader's eye if you only try it once every week or two weeks.

2. Teach students to use proper proofreader's symbols. Six key symbols are provided in this chapter. If your students are ready for more, check in any good dictionary (under proofreader) or in a good handbook. When you use editorial symbols, you teach students to work like professionals. (Students who aren't ready for this level can still check for their name, or to be sure they have included everything they wanted to include.)

3. Keep practice focused until students get pretty good at spotting errors. That is, put one kind of error in a line. Don't ask beginning editors to look for two, three, or four different kinds of things at once.

4. Ask students to work individually first, then to check with a partner, then to check with you for the answer. Ask them to compare their text with yours.

5. Do NOT ask students to edit each other's text. This task is much too hard for beginning editors (How many adult writers would you trust, really trust, to edit something you were going to publish?). It takes years of experience to prepare to do quality, final editing on the text of others. To put students in this position is stressful for the student editor, and unfair to the writer.

6. Ask students to practice on text that is **NOT THEIR OWN.** The hardest place to find an error is inside your own writing. Students need to <u>practice</u> first, then gradually transfer their skills to their own work.

7. Print **BIG.** The text here in our practice lessons is small for purposes of economy. But when you share lessons with students,

write big, and leave big spaces between words so students have plenty of room to insert editorial marks See how much easier this would be ?

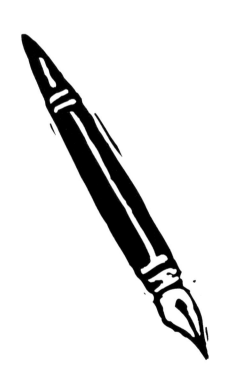

SAMPLE MINI-LESSONS

Lesson 1

Bob is here

bob is here.

Is Bob here

Is Bob heer ?

Lesson 1

Bob is here ⊙

bob is here.

Is Bob here

here

Is Bob heer?

Lesson 2

I love my dog

i love my dog.

I luv my dog.

I love my Dog.

Lesson 2

I love my dog ⊙

i love my dog.

love

I luv my dog.

I love my Dog.

Lesson 3

I lik to write.

I like too writte.

i like to Write.

I like to write

Lesson 3

e

I lik to write.

I like too writte.

i like to Write.

I like to write ⊙

161

Lesson 4

Who took my pencil

Whotook mypencil?

Who took took my pencil?

who took my pencil?

Lesson 4

Who took my pencil ?

Whotook mypencil?

Who took ~~took~~ my pencil?

who took my pencil?

Lesson 5

Stop hitting me?

Stop. Hitting me.

stop hitting me.

Stop hiting me.

Stop hitting mee.

Lesson 5

Stop hitting me?

Stop Hitting me.

stop hitting me.

Stop hiting me.

Stop hitting mee.

These lessons are only examples. Make up your own, using names or events known to your students. When they're ready, have them invent their own editing practice. Then, students can lead lessons, and you can play editor, too!

FOUR LAST REMINDERS

1. Let students do their own editing for publication to the extent they *can*. When they reach a point at which they need help, let them initiate the request. Then provide it. You can say, "You will be the <u>content editor</u>, in charge of deciding what you write about or draw. You will also be the <u>production editor</u>, deciding things like

   - What the title will be
   - What colors you will use
   - What fonts (if any) you will use
   - How long your publication will be
   - Whether you will use text or pictures or both

   Together, you and I will be the <u>copy editors</u> who check to see that everything is just correct and just the way you want it before your document is published.

2. No matter who does the editing (you, another student, the writer, a parent), make sure that person receives credit. Your credits can be listed this way:

   Author: _____

   Illustrator: _____

   Content editor: _____

   Production editor: _____

   Copy editor: _____

   More than one person can receive credit, if that is appropriate. Also, one person can do more than one job, and his or her name would then appear two or more times!

3. Give the writer <u>final approval</u>. In real life, a copy editor would never dream of sending a book to press without showing the writer what he or she had done, and requesting the writer's approval of all changes. Yet, seldom do we follow this simple policy of courtesy and respect for the writer's integrity in the classroom. We can, though, and we should. We often complain that students do not look at our editorial changes. True! They are more likely to look if we

- Keep the number of changes small, even if that means not correcting every last thing every time
- Ask student writers to approve our editing, not just accept it

4. <u>Don't edit everything</u>. Edit personal text when it's important (a favorite story the writer wants to publish, a significant letter, an important report). Otherwise, <u>practice</u> editing on short mini-lessons in which the writer has no vested interest. Then, he or she can develop a true copy editor's eye.

HELP WITH SPELLING

1. LISTS

Encourage students to invent their own word lists:
• Words I need to use a lot
• Words that are hard for me (personal list)
• Words I'm just curious about
• Sight words I want to learn

2. ASTERISKS ★★★★★★

Let student writers mark with an asterisk the **ONE WORD** (yes, just one) they **REALLY** want help with in a given piece of writing. Otherwise, ask them to use their best inventive spelling skills to make a good guess.

3. MINI-LESSONS

Practice as a group sounding out one, two, or more (up to five) words that students select.

4. READ, READ, READ ... & BORROW!

"I wish teachers wouldn't tell children not to worry about their spelling ... . What they should say is, 'When you write, try your best. Spelling words as best you can is helping your reader.'"

Mary Ellen Giacobbe, Grade 1 teacher
in Donald Graves, *A Fresh Look At Writing*, 255

THE 100 MOST COMMON WORDS IN ENGLISH WRITING

Words 1-25	Words 26-50	Words 51-75	Words 76-100
the	or	will	number
of	one	up	no
and	had	other	way
a	by	about	could
to	word	out	people
in	but	many	my
is	not	then	than
you	what	them	first
that	all	these	water
it	were	so	been
he	we	some	call
was	when	her	who
for	your	would	oil
on	can	make	now
are	said	like	find
as	there	him	long
with	use	into	down
his	an	time	day
they	each	has	did
I	which	look	get
at	she	two	come
be	do	more	made
this	how	write	may
have	their	go	part
from	if	see	over

For additional instant words, see <u>Spelling Book</u> by Edward Fly, Laguna Beach Educational Books, 245 Grandview, Laguna Beach, CA 92651 (1992).

MORE FOOD FOR THOUGHT

Since 1906, study after study has shown that knowledge of grammar fails to correlate with the ability to interpret literature, the ability to learn a foreign language, or, most important, the ability to write or speak well. One study showed that knowledge of grammar was more highly correlated with mathematical than verbal abilities.
Graves and Stuart, 175

To the untrained eye [inventive spelling] often looks like garbled spelling. Some parents fear that children will memorize their unconventional versions of words. Evidence shows, however, that those fears are unfounded.
Graves and Stuart, 171

Many highly intelligent and successful people, like John F. Kennedy, for example, [have been] poor spellers. Even some brilliant writers cannot spell. Few American novels have been held in higher regard than *The Great Gatsby*; yet Fitzgerald's handwritten manuscript for the classic reportedly contained no fewer than fifty-five hundred spelling errors.
Graves and Stuart, 167

It is voice in writing that conveys a sense of the writer's personality. In fiction, voice is one of the qualities that make a character or narrator convincing. A writer's voice can even give a business memo flavor and technical writing a touch of humanity.
Graves and Stuart, 38

Chapter 7

TEACHER TALK: ANSWERS TO TEN FREQUENTLY ASKED QUESTIONS

1. DO I REALLY NEED TO TEACH ALL SIX TRAITS AT PRIMARY LEVEL?

The most important thing to teach at this level is the **LANGUAGE** of the traits. If you read aloud to your students, this will happen quite naturally through the sharing of good literature and other writing samples (e.g., a travel brochure, text from a cookbook). The sooner young writers can begin thinking and speaking in "writers' language," the more quickly they will learn about writing and the easier it will be for them. If you want a point of focus, ideas and voice are good beginning traits: ideas because this trait prompts young writers to think, to focus on detail, to notice, to observe, and to think of personally important topics; and voice because to celebrate voice is to honor individuality and perspective. If your teaching environment is filled with print, you'll find yourself teaching conventions, too, like it or not—so, why not take advantage of young writers' insatiable curiosity to help them borrow meaningfully?

Keep in mind that <u>teaching</u> traits and <u>looking for evidence</u> of traits in your students' writing are **NOT** the same thing. Not at all! Student writers "tune in" to the traits as listeners and thinkers long, long before they are ready to reproduce those traits in their own work. They can **HEAR** fluency well before they can imitate it in their own work (and they can demonstrate it in their own dictated pieces). Similarly, they can predict endings to stories well before they've mastered the fine art of crafting a good conclusion themselves. The preceding chapter ("Teaching Traits to Primary Writers") offers many possibilities for linking traits and trait language to literature or other samples of writing.

2. DO I NEED TO USE THE SIX-TRAIT MODEL TO ASSESS EVERYTHING STUDENTS DO?

NO!!! Most definitely not. Assessing <u>everything</u>, especially using numbers, is not necessary or even helpful. Here are some good guidelines for sound assessment at primary level:

a) Don't assess everything.
It's too stressful for students and for you, and will probably limit the amount of writing you encourage. Let students do lots of practicing, experimenting, and playing with writing with no particular concern for assessment. Practice is vital. Keep it short and make it frequent. But don't feel compelled to assess.

b) Base assessment on descriptors.
Descriptors are language, language that defines growth—e.g., beginning writer, developing writer, fluent/experienced writer. If they're well written and clear, they can tell you more than numbers alone. Numbers and letter grades make more sense once the person being assessed can begin to interpret what those numbers or grades mean—not before.

c) Consider growth.

If your students keep portfolios, you'll see big changes from September to November to January ... March ... May. You may want that progress reflected in your assessment. Here's where a checklist can help: e.g., Perhaps growth in 10 areas shows more strength than growth in 6 areas or 2 areas, and so on. Amount of growth may be important, too; few things speak so loudly to parents about how much their student writers have achieved as actual samples collected at various times during the year. Be SURE students put dates on everything.

d) Record participation in the writing process

as part of your assessment. Everything need not be based on final products. You may wish to also give credit to the student who thinks up her own topics, does some brainstorming or talking or thinking before she writes, shares her writing or her art with others (students, a parent or other family or you), who shows some interest in revision—or even does some revision, who does a final editing check (for name on the paper, etc.), or simply asks good writer's questions (What is this mark of punctuation for? Where can I get information on frogs? What's another way to end besides THE END?).

e) Watch for experimentation.

Consider that completing writing or art projects, expressing a sense of joy in the writing process, playing with language, inventing words, organizing stories orally, borrowing from the environment, asking questions, and listening thoughtfully are all writing accomplishments in themselves.

f) Assess <u>completion</u> of tasks.

"I did it, I finished," is a big deal at primary level. Give credit for completion, and don't worry about evaluating the final product.

3. WHAT ABOUT CONVENTIONS?

Conventions are important, but they're not sacred. Unless, of course, we make them so! Isn't it interesting? We invented them, all of them, and now they control so much of what we do and how we think of one another! Pull the old curtain back, and see conventions for what they are: nothing more than consistencies people agree to abide by in order to make text easier to mentally process.

Like it or not, conventions are changing all the time, and this is one of the main reasons that even expert editors cannot agree among themselves about what is correct at any given moment. Of course, this does not mean that we do not need to pay attention to conventions. We do! Employers are asking for workers who can spell and punctuate. That's the reality. But we teach control of conventions better, faster, more effectively if we are realistic about goals, and if we let our students be the editors.

First, we need to recognize that "mastery of conventions," a phrase which appears often on lists of curriculum goals, is wholly unachievable. By anyone. Not even professional editors would aspire to anything so cosmically elusive; that's why their office shelves are lined with copy editors' source books, many dictionaries, punctuation guidebooks, and handbooks of all sorts. Tens of thousands of rules govern the use of conventions, many evolving even as I write this. We all need good references and skill in using them in order to make conventions strong.

What we really mean, of course, when we say "mastery of conventions" is a basic understanding of commonly used conventions of spelling, grammar, and punctuation sufficient to enable the writer to produce readable, socially acceptable business letters, reports, explanations, summaries, evaluations, and, possibly, analyses, critiques, or narratives. Still an imposing goal. Still a long-range goal.

To get there, we must begin with conventions appropriate to a writer's understanding, observations, and editing skill. That way, she (or he) can manage the editing process. So, do we begin with sophisticated conventions like correct spelling and punctuation? Of course not. Those will be our goals eventually, but at primary level, we must first teach the concept of conventional correctness.

To do this, we begin with what primary writers notice first: People make marks on a page to communicate. Those marks usually go left to right on the page. They have a definite shape. The big shapes (paragraphs, sentences, words) have little shapes (letters, punctuation) embedded within them. The shapes have a pattern. They have consistency. Some shapes go with sounds. Some marks (punctuation) give clues about meaning ... and so on.

Conventions which are appropriate at primary level can and should look a little different from those that are properly emphasized with older writers. It is quite appropriate to begin holding fourth- and fifth-graders accountable for some spelling and punctuation since these have been taught and students of this age have (we hope) some reading experience, and the skills to begin using written resources to look up what they do not know.

Primary writers are at a different place. They are still learning to hold and move pencils, to choose the paper and writing implements they will use, to decide just where on the paper to make that first mark, and so forth.

> Bees bees kan stng
>
> you nd thay .
>
> liv in the feld
>
> **Age 5**

Of course, they are noticing and applying conventions **ALL THE TIME**. We simply need to take a step back from semicolons, quotation marks and commas in a series and notice the conventions <u>primary writers</u> notice—and imitate.

Things like left-right orientation are not automatically programmed into a young writer's mind; all must be learned through observation or instruction. Students who begin school knowing that letters represent sound or knowing that writing normally goes from left to right on the page have already come quite a long way conventionally.

As students gain more practice writing, reading, and noticing the print in their environment, they begin to see and imitate more sophisticated conventions such as these:

- Margins

- Title placed at the top of the page

- Capitals at beginnings of sentences or lines on the page

- Punctuation at ends of sentences or lines on the page

- Capitals on names or important words

- Readable spelling with (1) beginning sounds represented, then (2) beginning & end sounds, then (3) most consonants, then (4) long vowels, then (5) most vowels

- Incorporation of such punctuation marks as ellipses, colons, semi-colons, quotation marks, & apostrophes in the text

It takes a long time and lots of observation to bring student writers to this point of awareness and experimentation with conventions. Correct application of spelling, grammatical structure, and punctuation will come with time, IF students have

- Many opportunities to create personal text they care about enough to edit

- A LOT of diverse & interesting environmental print (posters, books, magazines, etc.) to look through, read, & enjoy

- Many opportunities to listen to language used well (in conversation & oral reading)

4. DO STUDENTS NEED TO WRITE EVERY DAY?

Do readers need to read every day? Pitchers pitch every day? That depends on how good they want to get. How confident do you want your students to be? How natural do you want writing to feel?

Remember, of course, that you do not need to set aside a one-hour or half-hour "writing time" for everyday writing to occur. It can be interwoven with everyday activities. At primary level, writing must include such things as art, dictation, brainstorming, responding to literature, working with the teacher on his/her writing, and so forth.

*W*hen a teacher asks me,
"I can only teach writing one day a week. What kind of program should I have?" my response is, "Don't teach it at all. You will encourage poor habits in your students and they will only learn to dislike writing."

Donald Graves
A Fresh Look At Writing, 104

Further, writing includes not just stories, but also lists of rules, how-to pieces, explanations, notes, thank yous, labels, maps, personal responses, and other forms. Following are just a FEW ideas for the many ways you might incorporate writing into instruction throughout the day.

Everyday Writing Activities

a) As students come in, say, "I like to clear my head for the day by writing what I'm thinking. Today I'm feeling a little frustrated because the bus was late and it almost made me late. I'm going to write about that. What are you thinking about right now? What's on your mind? Take five minutes and write about it. Remember, you can use words or pictures in your writing."

b) Remember our visitor yesterday who talked to us about science? Let's compose a thank you note to let her know how much we enjoyed having her. I'll do the writing if you'll help me think what to say and how to begin.

c) Some people have been saying we need new rules for our playground. Let's talk about that and we'll write down the rules you think are important.

d) Did you enjoy that story? (movie?) I'd like you to write your response to include in your journal. You can use words or pictures or both.

e) (At the end of a math, social studies, science, etc., lesson) What was the most important thing you learned in the last 15 minutes? Take a minute to talk about that with a partner, then write what you learned.

f) Today we planted radishes. Let's make some predictions about what will happen by next Friday at this time—that's a week away. Use words or pictures to write what you predict.

g) Conferences will happen next week. Let's put together some invitations that will make your family or a friend of your choice feel welcome to come.

h) Let's pretend we're going to have a picnic right here at the school. We have $40 to spend on the food. Help me make a list of things we should buy—then we'll figure up the cost.

l) Last week the phone company made a mistake on my phone bill. They overcharged me by $5. I want to write them a letter to get this taken care of. Help me put my letter together.

j) I am in charge of an after-school meeting of teachers this week, and I need to send everyone a memo reminding them to come. I want your help planning what I should write. What kinds of things should I be sure to include in my memo do you think?

Writing is as much a part of everyday life as reading. Students learn to be proficient writers in a wide range of situations when their help and opinions are regularly sought. Writing isn't just pushing a pencil across paper; it's all the thinking and planning that goes on ahead of time, too. Even the youngest of writers can help with that part!

In order to help children develop as writers, we need to share in the writing process by being writers ourselves. By providing demonstrations of writing in action, by being partners in the creating process, we do more to help children figure out how to be writers themselves than all of our correcting of their "mistakes" can ever hope to accomplish.

Judith Newman
The Craft of Children's Writing, 72

---

5. WHAT GOES ON IN WRITER'S WORKSHOP?

The purpose of writer's workshop is to allow students to work in their own ways and at their own pace. It might <u>look</u> chaotic or haphazard, but a good writer's workshop is very organized and purposeful while allowing lots of individual freedom.

TO BEGIN

Start with everyone together in a group. A good way to begin is to ask, "What will you be working on today?" If your class is small, you can allow students to answer individually. If you have a bigger group, a show of hands will do. Also ask, "How many are still finding a topic? Who is working on a picture or a paper? Who is ready to share? Who is ready for a new topic? Who has a question you need help with?" You can, if you wish, form small groups of students working on similar tasks.

MEANWHILE, WHAT SHOULD <u>YOU</u> BE DOING??

As students work, you roam. Have mini-conferences: "You're including labels on your picture this time .... Where did you get your idea for a story about spaghetti? .... There is so much feeling in this picture .... I love the colors you chose to show the storm in the sky! .... I notice you're putting more periods in your writing now. Tell me about that."

> Writers sometimes hear their own voices best when they talk. Teachers can help small children develop their voices by allowing them to talk a lot.
>
> Graves and Stuart, 1985, p. 104

ARE THERE ANY RULES HERE??

Sure. Rules help keep things orderly, and remind students how they should be spending their time. Here are possibilities—these are simple, and even nonreaders can remember them:

- **Work on writing**

- **Use quiet voices**

- **"Writing talk" only**

- **Help each other if I'm busy**

TIME TO CLOSE

You may want to gather students for closure, too. It's a nice time to sit in a circle and talk about how much you got done and how you went about it: How many came up with a topic? Did anyone answer a writing question for somebody? Does anyone have a question that didn't get answered? Does anyone want to share his or her writing?

I kan . run .
For aBowt.formils.

6. HOW DO I KNOW WHEN STUDENTS ARE SUCCESSFUL?

This question seems to lead us right back to assessment, but improved quality of the final product isn't the only measure of success in writing. Ask first, do your students enjoy writing? If the answer is yes, you and they are successful. <u>Wanting to write</u> is a **HUGE** indicator of success.

Other things to look for:

- ♥ Students are beginning to take some steps independently, moving beyond a "Now what do I do?" approach.
- ♥ Students are beginning to help one another solve the problems writers face.
- ♥ Students are spending more time on individual pieces.
- ♥ Writing & pictures include more details.
- ♥ Signs of voice are stronger—more individuality, more expression.
- ♥ Students are asking more writer's questions.
- ♥ Students are experimenting—trying new things.
- ♥ Students are asking, "When will we write?"
- ♥ Samples within a portfolio show growth over time.
- ♥ Students are using the language of writers—talking about things like ideas, details, beginnings & endings, words, voice, conventions.

7. DO STUDENTS NEED TO REVISE EVERYTHING THEY WRITE?

Certainly not. Who on earth would want to do that? At primary level, the most important goal is helping your students to know what revision is. How do you make that happen? The best way is to <u>model</u> it, rather than assign it—e.g.,

> Remember last week when I wrote that poem about the flower garden? When I read it again this morning, I thought it was a little too short. I left out an important part, so today I added that. I'd like to read both versions to you and see what you think . . . .

When you model revision, but do NOT require it, students begin to see revision as an empowering process, which it is. Revision is the writer's privilege, not the writer's curse. As you model, make it look manageable, small even. Revision is repulsive to beginning students MOSTLY because the task of "doing it all over" (which many think of as revision) looks so

It's a big writing event. Show your writers that revision can be as simple as crossing out, adding a word or detail to a picture. For a primary writer, adding a small detail is a BIG step in revision. It's enough. And it certainly does not need to happen with every piece.

Above all, emphasize revision is not <u>redoing</u>. Revision is "seeing again" with new eyes—preferably after a little time has gone by. How do you revise? By putting on your reader's hat for a little while, thinking like a reader, asking, "What else would I like to know? What's not clear yet?"

So, what's the best way to teach revision to young writers? Having them pick up their pencils and revise? NO!!! By **READING** to them often, and asking them to think about what you read. To think like <u>readers</u>. Isn't that how we learn the process, after all? As teachers, we read our students' work. We react. We see what has to be done. Then, too often, we assign the "doing" to our students. They're not ready! They haven't gone through the same reflective process. You must read first. Think, reflect, and question.

Remember the visualizing exercise from the section on writing process? Put it to work following a specific writing activity. Suppose the class has drawn a mural following a visit to the zoo. You might say, "**OK**, we think our mural is about done. It has lots of detail. But before we stop, let's make sure there's nothing more we want to add. Close your eyes for just a minute and picture yourself back at the zoo. Really try to <u>see</u> it, <u>hear</u> it, <u>smell</u> the zoo smells . . . . Now ask yourself, 'Is there any little detail we missed that we should add?'"

8. Is it important for me to write with my students?

YES. Oh, yes. So much can be gained from modeling that it is impossible to overstate the importance of letting students <u>see</u> you as a writer, in many contexts. First—and perhaps most important—you can let them see you think writing is important, and sometimes difficult but still do-able, and often fun.

> If you are not a writer,
> you will not understand the difficulties of writing. If you are not a writer, you will not know the fears and hopes of the writers you teach. If you are not a writer, you will not be aware of the needs of writers: needs such as a real purpose for writing; a real response to writing; a real knowledge about grammar, spelling, and punctuation to make writing correct.
>
> *Mem Fox*
> <u>Radical Reflections</u>, 163

Second, your young writers have a chance to see you in the many different roles writers play for after all. Writing, like reading, differs according to purpose, audience, topic, and situation. Sometimes you are a creative writer, sometimes a reporter, sometimes one friend writing to another, sometimes a member of the community, sometimes a cook sharing a recipe, or the recipient of a gift sharing a thank you.

In each case, you can show

- ♥ **How you plan your writing**
- ♥ **How you come up with a topic**
- ♥ **How you think about audience**
- ♥ **How you choose the right words**

♥ How you know if you need to revise
♥ What to do if you can't spell a word
♥ When to ask for help

... and your thinking on many, many other decisions that make writing work. What you share when you write is not just the writing itself—already a treasure, no matter how good or bad it is!—but the story of your process, the story of HOW. That is invaluable. Students learn a little by seeing the products of writing; they learn worlds by seeing the process.

9. MY STUDENTS ARE SO YOUNG. MANY AREN'T READY TO WRITE ON THEIR OWN. WHAT DO I DO?

Remember that they do not need to produce conventional written text to begin writing. They can write though pictures or dictation, or on audiotape. They can listen to the writing of others as you share stories and articles.

Writing takes many forms, and as soon as students can speak, they are ready to begin at some level, in some form. As they watch you write, advise you on word choice or ideas, they are participating in the writing process. Dictated pieces often show a complexity of ideas that won't reveal itself through self-generated written text for months or even years. But complexity of thinking is what writing is all about. Capture it. Students do not need to dictate every piece, but they <u>should dictate sometimes</u> so we can see and appreciate their thinking a bit more closely than written text allows.

10. WHAT ARE THE MOST IMPORTANT SKILLS & IDEAS I CAN GIVE MY YOUNG WRITERS?

♥ **Belief that writing is an adventure**

♥ **Courage to experiment**

♥ **Trust in their own personal voice**

♥ **A writer's language to use in thinking, learning, & reflecting**

♥ **Skill in asking helpful questions**

♥ **A sense that the best topics are connected to one's own life experiences & passions**

♥ **An understanding of the difference between editing & revising**

♥ **Belief that when writing doesn't work out the way you planned, you can still learn from it—& it will be better tomorrow!**

Chapter 8

USING READING TO TEACH WRITING

In order to write well, we must learn to think like readers. Writers wear two hats, really. On the one hand, they are creating, generating, shaping text. On the other, they are asking, "Who is my audience? What do my readers already know about this topic? What do they need to know? What will interest them? What will keep them here, spending time with me, instead of running off to do something else?"

How does a writer answer these questions? From experience. Experience as a <u>reader</u>.

When writers draft, they begin to bring shape to the written piece. Concern focuses on information, purpose, audience, organization, and choice of language. I suggest that the reader deals with the same concepts. What effect does the writer want? What has the author accomplished? Students need experience in recognizing purpose. They should be helped to develop internalized story grammars. They need to understand the "why's" behind language selection.

Charles Chew

Breaking Ground, 171

The value of reading aloud

As you share written text aloud to your students, you are, in fact, teaching them to write. This is true because writing is more than moving a pencil. Writing is thinking, thinking like a writer, and equally important, like a reader. As students begin to read to and for themselves, they have opportunities, with your encouragement, to begin asking good reader's questions. These questions will later guide them as writers. So, read aloud often—from the most wonderfully written, exciting, passionate, vivid, colorful, and engaging texts you can find. (Now and then, throw in a dud, just to let your students hear and comment on the difference. It's all part of learning to think like a writer.)

Some Books You & Your Students Will Love

In this section, you'll find some old favorites and some beautiful new recommendations for your read-aloud library. Don't feel restricted by this short list, however! Take Mem Fox's advice and "read aloud, alive, a lot!"

> Powerful writers and powerful speakers have two wells they can draw on for that power: one is the well of rhythm; the other is the well of vocabulary. But vocabulary and a sense of rhythm are almost impossible to "teach" in the narrow sense of the word. So how are children expected to develop a sense of rhythm or a wide vocabulary? By being read to, alive, a lot!
>
> *Mem Fox*
>
> *Radical Reflections*, 68

Then she went back home with the honey.

BOOKS TO BUILD OBSERVATION SKILLS

📖 Blizzard, Gladys S. Come Look With Me. 1992. Thomasson-Grant. ISBN 0-56566-013-7.

This sumptuously illustrated book takes advantage of children's natural fascination with animals to take them on a marvelous tour of the art world, from cave paintings to African and Asian paintings to a very modern looking snail by Matisse. You and your students will have fun exploring the paintings together, especially under the guidance of very well-crafted questions that accompany each painting, and invite young eyes to look well within. Of the cave painting, the author asks, "Which animals look the strongest and most powerful? How did the artist make it look that way? Why do you think the artist painted some animals right over others?" Answer these very intriguing questions, then let students come up with some of their own.

Don't be intimidated!

The language of the text is sophisticated. So is the fluency. Do not let this inhibit you for a moment. The descriptions and histories are clear and beautifully written, and when you read text that's a little bit of a stretch, you help your students develop vocabulary and an ear for sentence fluency and construction they can achieve no other way.

Follow-up activity

For even more fun, encourage your young writers/artists to pose a question about their next piece of art work. They can dictate their questions, then present them to parents during a conference, art fair, or back to school visit.

What kind of writing is that?

Ask your students, "What kind of writing is this?" It's <u>expository</u>—or, you may wish to call it <u>informational</u> (writing that explains). Parts are <u>narrative</u>, too (writing that tells a story). This writer includes brief <u>biographies</u> (the story of a person's life) of many of the artists whose work is represented. You can use this book to help your students understand each of these terms.

Additional questions

- Can pictures have as much voice as writing? How do you know?
- How do artists put voice in their work?
- Are details important in a picture? Why?
- Do pictures sometimes teach you things?

Johnson, Stephen T. <u>Alphabet City</u>. 1995. Viking. ISBN 0-670-85631-2.

How closely do you look at the world all around us? Did you ever notice the letter "Z" in a fire escape, the "X" in the infrastructure of a bridge, the "Q" in a train wheel, the "E" in the profile of a semaphore? This book takes a sharp-eyed and playful look at the intriguing shapes all around us, inviting us to do the same.

Begin by having students find the letters within the book itself. You may wish to make colored overheads, or laminated pages you can shuffle and sort. That way, you can share them out of order, or ask students to put them into alphabetical order, thereby adding to the challenge!

Next steps

Now, look around your classroom. Find more letters ... numbers, too. Where are they buried? Where are they hiding? Sketch one or two.

Want more alphabet adventure?

Invite students to explore the school grounds, nearby ball fields, city blocks, shopping centers, wetlands, meadows, pathways, whatever ... a room at home, the profile of a city street, a suburban roadway or park. Let them come up with their own letter sketches. Let others find the letters within each child's sketch. Make a book of your own!

📖 Wick, Walter and Marzollo, Jean. <u>I Spy: A Book of Picture Riddles</u>. 1996. Scholastic. ISBN 0-590-46295-4.

You'll have more fun than you can imagine testing your visual powers on these intriguing and quirky pictures. If you make color copies and laminate them, you can divide the fun by putting students into groups to see who can find things first. Are your students readers? If so, you can make written lists of things to look for (simplifying the lists in the book to make reading easier) and let different groups work on different pictures.

Following up

Let students create a group picture, with each child hiding one or two "secrets" within. Remember to make a list of the "buried treasures." This will call for some good inventive spelling strategies, and a little editorial help (perhaps) on your part. Great way to combine details (ideas) and conventions.

BOOKS FOR DEVELOPING A SENSE OF PLACE

How much do landscapes influence our thoughts, feelings, views of the world? Who knows? But what a fascinating topic to explore, this topic of place. Where we live, where we feel centered, where we feel at home. Special places, we soon discover, are not the Disneylands and parade grounds of the world, but the quiet corners special and known to each of us. The following books invite students to explore this theme in a variety of ways.

📖 Angelou, Maya. <u>My Painted House, My Friendly Chicken and Me</u>. 1994. Clarkson N. Potter (Random House). ISBN 0-517-59667-9.

Want to explore the power of photo journalism? Layout? Color and type variation? Treat your eyes to this visual explosion of ideas, colors, shapes, and images. Text and photos alternately carry the story, and both are alive, whimsical, and given to sudden and delightful shifts in personality. This is a book of visual surprises which depicts, through the eyes of eight-year-old Thandi, the diverse and delightful culture of an Ndebele village in South

Africa. Come visit. Meet the friendly chicken. The squirmy brother, too. See traditional native beadwork and wall murals blend with modern street lamps and school uniforms. Let your imagination soar amid the multiple patterns of life.

Then ...

Try a photo journal of your own! You might include current photos of your students, pictures of younger (or older) siblings, pets, parents, grandparents, places of interest in your community. Write or dictate labels, statements, questions, paragraphs, reflective thoughts to connect the photos.

Think about dividing tasks

Why not have some students write, some edit, some work on layout? Don't be afraid to add colors, varying fonts and sizes. Experiment. Be daring!

Bruchac, Joseph and Locker, Thomas. Between Earth & Sky: Legends of Native American Sacred Places. 1996. Harcourt Brace & Company. ISBN 0-15-200042-9.

This is a reverent and graceful text that explores sacred places from seven directions: east, west, north, south, above, below, within. Rhythmic text captures the legends of many Native American people, celebrating their sacred places. Those places are also gloriously depicted in soft watercolors that honor the beauty, color, and spirit of the earth itself.

Read the text as an excellent example of fluency, just enjoying the gentle rhythms and the richness of the language.

For a bit of geographic history

How many of your students know where in the U.S. any of the original Native nations lived? You might make some guesses, based on the text, then check your guesses against the map in the back of this book.

Further exploration

Have some questions about the lives or culture of Native people? Make a list of questions and explore, through further reading, interviews, Internet, etc.

📖 MacLachlan, Patricia. <u>All the Places to Love</u>. 1994. Harper Collins. ISBN 0-06-021098-2.

The beautiful water colors in this book invite students to share their own sense of place through art. Try this. Before sharing the book, ask students to make (with you) a list of places that are really special to them. Remember that a place can be as tiny as the corner of a room, the nook of a tree, a pocket, a treasure chest, a favorite chair. It doesn't have to be a big, glitzy, splashy, public place. Think small. Think personal.

Now share the book, asking students to notice how each person has a slightly different "place to love." Why is that? What makes a place special to someone?

Now, describe <u>your</u> special places, using text, art, or both. Let students dictate, create poems, make audiotapes, or draw pictures—whatever works here. Make a collection, perhaps a book.

In addition ...

you might ask students to do a short oral presentation, perhaps in small groups, to talk about their special places and why they chose as they did.

Ask students to interview one other person outside of the class about that person's "special place." What do they discover? Do we all like different things? Are there certain common characteristics of special places?

MacLachlan, Patricia. <u>What You Know First</u>. 1995. Harper Collins. ISBN 0-06-024413-5.

Beautiful, soft-toned woodcut prints give an old-time, nostalgic look to this book of memories and anticipation. With characteristic sensitivity, Patricia MacLachlan explores a theme which haunts many young people: the difficulty of moving to a new place. What will it be like? How will you bear to say good-bye? What will you take to ease the heartache and keep the memories forever alive? Before reading, you might ask if any of your students have moved. Have any moved more than once? Who has moved the farthest? The shortest distance? What was the best thing about moving? What was hardest? Give students opportunities to tell stories of moving, in words or pictures.

Building some organizational skills
As a follow-up, ask students what they think will happen after the writer's move. What will it be like? What will the writer remember? Will the new place feel "right?" Use words or pictures to look into the future.

Hearing the writer's voice
The teller of this tale does NOT want to move! How do you know this? Does she express her feelings strongly?

Other suggestions
Suppose students were going to move next year or next month. What might they take with them to remember your neighborhood, community, town or school? What things make special connections (like the twig and the little bag of dirt in the story)? You can't take the sky perhaps, but what could you take to <u>remind</u> you of the sky?

Moving doesn't always have to mean going to a new town. We move all the time, don't we? From grade to grade, for instance. Ask what students might take with them next year to remind them of kindergarten or first grade or ... whatever. Make a collection.

Photographs

Photos hold special memories. Why? You might ask students each to bring in one photograph to make a memory collection. Sketches work, too.

Stories

help others share in the "good old days" they're too young to have lived for themselves. Ask students to find, if possible, a parent, grandparent, other relative, or older neighbor who will share one story of the "good old days." They can retell stories in small groups of three. If there's enough interest, you can generate a timeline or scrapbook of "Good Old Days Stories."

Ryder, Joanne. Earthdance. 1996. Henry Holt. ISBN 0-8050-2678-9.

Joanne Ryder is the 1995 recipient of the American Nature Study Society's Award for Children's Science Literature. You'll see why when you dance your way through this melodious, joyous celebration of the Earth. Young, energetic readers/listeners love this one because they can act it out. They actually become the Earth. Yes. They imagine themselves spinning, spinning through space, their hair becoming the trees and mountains and grass, voice becoming the crackling of the great icebergs. It's a simple and energetic version of reader's theater.

Read it once for the message and rhythmic flow. It's poetic. Then read again while students act out the message, rotating, carrying the inhabitants of Earth gently through space.

Follow-up

How does Earth look close up? From far away? Farther yet? The distance of space? Ask students to pick a perspective, super close, pretty close, far away, farther yet, and sketch their versions of Earth as it might look from each distance. Create a collage or zoom-in, zoom-out series from the results.

What you know now

How long does it take the Earth to rotate on its axis? How do you know? How long is it light this time of year in northern Alaska? Where you live? At the equator? Is it different? How do you know? What if the earth did not rotate? What would happen to the oceans? The continents? To us?

Think up your own questions about the Earth. Then, plan a trip to your library (or browse the Internet) to find some answers—or you can bring resources (books, newspapers, journal articles, visitors, films) into your own classroom. Ask each pair of students to research ONE question.

BOOKS FOR DEVELOPING A SENSE OF SELF

Angelou, Maya. <u>Life Doesn't Frighten Me.</u> 1993. Random House. ISBN 1-55670-288-4.

What an excellent example of fluency this is! It is, indeed, a poem, which also reads like a story, and a protest, and a confession, and an autobiography. The paintings of Jean-Michel Basquiat simply sing with voice. They are a combination of graffiti, children's whimsy and spontaneity, cave paintings, nightmares come to life, and fairy tale illustrations, all rolled into one. They have a flavor and style all their own. The author is fearless (or is she?) in the face of life's many challenges.

Life <u>can</u> be scary

This can be a touchy and sensitive subject, but if you focus on the everyday challenges, and on your students' strategies for handling them, it's possible to deal with this important subject yet not be intrusive. Children do fear many things, from dreams to war to floods and earthquakes, snakes, mean dogs, drowning, rejection, public speaking, getting lost and … well, you name it. But in their writing, they (and we) can celebrate their bravery in coping with the fears we all face. If this is a topic you think your class might handle, you can create a powerful collection of writings, statements, or drawings which are guaranteed to ring with voice. (How does the writer in Angelou's book deal with fear?)

Have <u>you</u> (as teacher/writer) written anything in a while?

What scares <u>you</u>? Heights? Deep water? Staff meetings? (Just kidding.) Getting lost in the city? Driving on the freeway? Speaking to big groups? Write a poem or story about it. Ask students to help you plan, revise, and edit, then to illustrate your book for you. Ask them to help work on layout, too. Which fonts should you use? How big? Where should the title go? What color should the cover be? Choose five or six key illustrations and publish your poem or story, complete with credit to your student reviewers, editors, and illustrators! (Don't forget illustrations for front and back covers, too!)

Baylor, Byrd. <u>Guess Who My Favorite Person Is</u>. 1977. Macmillan. ISBN 0-689-71052-6.

This book is nearly 20 years old now, and it's as fresh, new, and wonderful as when it first came out. Such is the mark of a writer who seems to see right inside the human spirit. This is a book that truly celebrates individuality. We all like different things, don't we? What's your favorite color? Favorite smell? Thing to touch? Let students make personal lists. Then . . . .

Read the book, enjoying the great story, but also noticing how Baylor makes every detail specific and important. Not just blue, but "the blue on a lizard's belly. That sudden kind of blue you see just for a second sometime—so blue that afterwards you always think you made it up." Ah, yes—<u>that</u> blue. You can picture it, can't you? See if your students can get this specific about favorite colors, sounds, smells, things to touch, things that move, things that wiggle, or whatever. They can create their descriptions with pictures, words, or both.

Celebrate the range of favorites

Not everyone likes the very same colors, sounds, smells, etc. That's where individuality comes in. And individuality means voice!

Look again

Notice the creative layout of this text. See how short the lines are? Often

just a word

or two

like

this

running

down the

page.

See how

easy

this

makes reading

for

young eyes?

Your students can do this, too! They can write short lines with BIG print, making their own stories easier to read back next time. Format is important!

📖 Krull, Kathleen. <u>Wilma Unlimited</u>. 1996. Harcourt Brace & Company. ISBN 0-15-201267-2.

I would have bought this book just for the font. Really. It's Ariel, created by artist/photographer David Diaz. You may wish to point this out to students, who are likely to want to spend some time just playing with the shape and look of letters, after taking a close look at Diaz's creative masterpiece. Happily, you can treasure this book not only for the font, but for the superb illustrations and the dynamic, well-crafted story. As the title suggests, Krull tells the tale of the legendary Wilma Rudolph, who was told before age five that polio had paralyzed her left leg, and she would never walk again. Wilma, with courage that will give you chills, determines not only to walk but to run, and run she does, across the Olympic finish line and into history, the first woman to win three Olympic gold medals at a single Olympics. You'll cheer right along with the crowd. Share this fine text as a good story, a bit of history, or both.

Follow-up writing

Have students ever tried to do something very hard? To overcome a defeat or setback? Have you? Tell your stories, orally or through text or pictures.

Research

How much training do athletes do for the Olympics? Find out! Choose a favorite event and draw a picture connected to that event. Then, look up some information to go with your picture. Good research usually begins with a question, so ... make a list:

- What famous people have participated or won medals in this event?

- What kind of training must athletes do to participate?

- Who is the youngest (or oldest) person ever to win a medal in this event?

Participate!

Stage an "Olympics" of your own as part of PE. Make posters to advertise it. Later, take photos or draw sketches of events. Write up the results as if they were going to appear in the newspaper.

How did it feel?

Ask students how it might have felt to be Wilma and to get the news that she might not walk again. How did she react? How did Wilma feel 20 years later, racing across that finish line, the crowd roaring? Students might create a journal entry, written or dictated, or a picture (before and after) to express Wilma's moments of defeat and triumph. Before-and-after pictures are excellent for developing a sense of both comparative and chronological organization.

Ringgold, Faith. <u>Tar Beach</u>. 1991. Crown Publishers. ISBN 0-517-58030-6.

<u>Tar Beach</u> is more than a story. It's a quilt, too (actually on display at the Solomon R. Guggenheim Museum in New York City). It's also a slice of history, an autobiography, and a celebration of African-American culture and literature. Briefly, it tells the story of Cassie Louise Lightfoot, an eight-year-old child, who dreams of flying to freedom over the rooftops, over the George Washington Bridge. It is the story of all who yearn to fly free with their dreams. Ringgold's pictures are as magical as her text. She truly flies, and you will fly with her.

Listen, then ...

Ask students to sketch their own version before they look at Ringgold's own pictures. Make a "quilt" of their collection, and weave the text around it to resemble the quilt shown in the back of the book.

Or ...

ask students to interview older relatives or friends about dreams or wishes they might have had. Tell the stories or draw pictures to tell the tales.

Make a paper hopes & dreams quilt

Base it on sketches of the dreams, wishes, and hopes your students have for their own futures. Where would they like their "flights" to take them five, 10, or 20 years from now?

Books for Exploring the Concept of Story

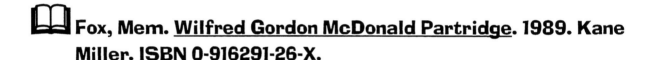

📖 Fox, Mem. <u>Wilfred Gordon McDonald Partridge</u>. 1989. Kane Miller. ISBN 0-916291-26-X.

A good story always has memorable characters and some tension—perhaps a decision to make or a problem to overcome, a journey to begin or complete. In this case, the characters are two people who, by the end of the story, will know more of each other and of themselves: a small boy named Wilfred Gordon McDonald Partridge, and an elderly woman named Miss Nancy, who lives in an old people's home next door. The problem: Miss Nancy has lost her memory. Wilfred Gordon would love to help, only he isn't altogether sure what a memory is or how you help someone recover it. Do <u>you</u> know? How <u>do</u> we remember things? What helps <u>you</u> remember? You might ask your students this. Also ask, "Can very young people and very old people be good friends? What do you think?"

Then share this wonderful story of friendship, memories, and treasures of the heart that keep us linked to the moments of our life.

Follow-up

Assemble your own collection of treasures: seashells, balls of various sorts, toys, photographs, feathers, birds' nests, twigs and dried flowers, books, whatever. Build connections. What memories do they hold? Capture the memories if you like with audio or video tape, writing, sketches, etc.

Solve a problem

Ask students to write individual stories in which the hero solves a problem, or write one together as a class. How does solving a problem give focus to your story?

On the subject of friendships

Use the text to explore the concept of unpredicted friendships. Have your students ever had a friend who was a lot older? Younger? From another part of the world? One who spoke a different language? Perhaps a friend who was not a person! Use pictures and/or text to explore the theme of unexpected (but treasured) friendships.

Lobel, Arnold. <u>Fables</u>. 1980. Harper Collins. ISBN 0-06-443046-4.

Can you trust a cat—if you're a fish? Can you find the end of the rainbow? Does it matter if you listen to your children as long as you're <u>there</u>? Are table manners really <u>that</u> important? These and a dozen other questions of life are neatly and skillfully addressed by the one and only Arnold Lobel in typical frank and humorous fashion. You'll enjoy these fables, too. Lobel writes with the adult reader and the young listener in mind, and you'll love the wry twists and the irony. These are real life fairy tales, and they have bite. Use them to show students that good stories make a point. They don't just drift along meaninglessly till the story teller runs out of breath. So you can ask, "What do you think is the point of that story? What is this writer trying to tell us?"

Here comes the mail!

When you've read two or three of these fables, set up a mail service to let students write to each other in character. For instance, what might Father Elephant say to the vain Mr. Bear who must dress in his finest coat just to go to town? What advice would the Hen have for the two Duck Sisters? What if the Fox and Wolf could have a chat? Would they like each other? Suppose the Hippopotamus and the Pelican had lunch? Who would pay? Who would do the dishes?

Lobel, Arnold. <u>The Frog and Toad Treasury</u>. 1970. Harper Collins. ISBN 0-06-026788-7.

Were there ever two more lovable characters than Frog and Toad? It's one thing to write <u>War and Peace</u> and tidy up all the little details of plot. But, good grief, Lobel does it over and over in the space of a few pages. Frog and Toad deal with laziness, embarrassment, misunderstanding, depression, spring fever, rejection, loneliness, and a host of other daily onslaughts. And through it all, their friendship blossoms. These are important and universal themes, the stuff of good writing. And they're tenderly, eloquently handled. The underlying question is always, "OK, how will Frog and Toad get out of this one?"

So, read, enjoy, laugh, sigh, cry, and then . . . .

Invent

a Frog and Toad tale of your own, individually or as a class.

Draw

pictures of Frog and Toad in the midst of their adventures.

Write

- A postcard Toad might like to receive when he's feeling lonely
- Or, a diary entry Frog might make
- Or, a recipe you might find in Toad's kitchen
- Or, a list of things to do either one might make up
- Or, a birthday "wish list" one or the other might write
- Or, a note from Toad to Frog on any subject

📖 Mathers, Petra. <u>Sophie and Lou</u>. 1991. Harper Collins.
ISBN 0-06-443331-5.

Painfully shy Sophie cannot face going to the Bookmobile; the librarian is so <u>tall!</u> How does it feel to be this shy? Lou knows. He sympathizes. Though we don't know this in the beginning. For a time, Sophie struggles with her shyness alone, and does quite well too, thank you. She learns to dance, and it's like Cassie Lightfoot learning to fly. It frees her! Young readers can applaud Sophie's courage, and appreciate Lou's compassion and friendliness, too. This is truly a fine and tender love story.

So, what happens next?
Write a sequel, in pictures or in text. Where will Sophie and Lou dance off to next?

Sophie's Diary
What's going on in Sophie's heart and mind during her shy period? Record her thoughts.

Or, Lou's Diary
For that matter, what does Lou think when he first sees Sophie? When does he first see her anyhow? Better look again. Hey, isn't that Lou hiding in the corner of that picture?

Exploring Shyness
Lots of people, including famous people, are painfully shy. Are you shy? Have you ever known someone who is? Write or tell a story about shyness.
Or, write a note explaining to a friend how to cope with shyness. Can you offer <u>two</u> good tips?

Discussion

Why are people shy? What if someone in your class were very shy, and you wanted to help? What could you do to make life easier for that person?

📖 Polacco, Patricia. <u>The Keeping Quilt</u>. 1988. Simon & Schuster. ISBN 0-671-64963-9.

A story of family love, tradition, heritage, and history. The keeping quilt is, by turns, a scarf, babushka, Sabbath tablecloth, wedding canopy, and receiving quilt for a newborn child—then, finally, an imaginary tent in the "Amazon jungle." Watch how it takes on new shapes, colors, and stitches through the years, and always, how it is treasured. What is the meaning behind such a treasure? Why do we hand things down to our children or grandchildren?

Follow-up

This wonderful story could be followed by a discussion of generational gifts. Perhaps your students (or their parents or friends) have gifts handed down from another generation. What stories go with those gifts? Tell them in poetry, prose, or pictures; or tell them orally.

Color & layout

Notice how the quilt catches your eye in every picture, as vibrant color flashes against the otherwise soft charcoal backgrounds of the historical sketches. What difference does color make? What does the artist's use of color say to readers in this story? Ask students to use color in a special way to make a point or make one part of a picture stand out.

📖 Polacco, Patricia. <u>Chicken Sunday</u>. 1992. Philomel Books.
   ISBN 0-399-22133-6.

Have you ever gotten into trouble for something you did not do? You might pose that question prior to reading this tale of love, sacrifice, courage and creativity. Beautiful, passionately conceptualized folk art illustrations grace this tale of three ingenious little spirits who make dreams come true for Miss Eula, the woman with a voice "like slow thunder and sweet rain." You have to relish word choice like that. Polacco has a gift for making everyday words shine like jewels. This is a story you'll likely want to read more than once.

Chutzpah!

What is it? Mr. Kadinski says that the children in this story have "great chutzpah." What does he mean? Define this word using a story of your own or a picture that shows someone with <u>chutzpah</u>.

Make it a habit: Choose one or two new words from each story you explore together. Guess how to spell the word. Guess what it might mean. Record your guesses to see who comes closest. Then, look it up. As <u>soon</u> as students are able to do the looking up of new words, let them. Till then, model the looking-up process, telling them aloud what you are doing as you page through the dictionary .... "Let's see, <u>chutzpah</u> starts with a <u>c</u>, even though it sounds as if it should start with an <u>h</u>. What's the next letter?"

📖 Steig, William. <u>Amos & Boris</u>. 1977. Puffin Books.
   ISBN 0-14-050229-7.

I could have chosen any Steig book to fill this slot, really. Steig is a master of fine language, well used, and of lyrical, fluent prose that virtually dances over the page. What an ear. But this is my favorite among his many fine books for the quality of its story. It has one of the best plots in literature: two crises, both affecting characters about whom we care very much.

Resolution comes only with sacrifice and cooperation, and the ending isn't easy. It's hopeful, but realistic. You have to bite your lip a little. Amos and Boris are both courageous; neither is perfect. The dialogue is wonderful, the sentence structure glorious: "One night, in a phosphorescent sea, he [Amos] marveled at the sight of some whales spouting luminous water; and later, lying on the deck of his boat gazing at the immense, starry sky, the tiny mouse Amos, a little speck of a living thing in the vast living universe, felt thoroughly akin to it all." Who else (other than Carl Sagan) writes with such grace? *Phosphorescent ... marveled ... spouting ... luminous ... immense ... vast ... akin ....* What do these beautiful words mean? Have fun making some guesses. Then, make posters to illustrate just this <u>one vivid line</u>. Read the story through several times to enjoy the language, the fine phrasing, the resonant voice. Reprint it in BIG words, so students can begin to follow along. Let students who are ready read short parts aloud: a <u>word</u>, a phrase, a <u>tiny</u> bit of dialogue, or (for those who can) <u>more</u>!

Tuning in

Ask students to identify a favorite phrase or two. Make a list. Listening for favorite words is a good way to build listening skills.

Will they meet again?

What do you think? Will Amos and Boris meet again? You might pose this question to students, and see what answers they come up with. If they do meet, what might be the circumstances? How old might they be? What might happen?

Notice the colors

Notice how the sea changes colors in the pictures of this book. Why do you suppose that is? Do colors have moods? Can a color suggest danger? Or happiness? Talk about this with your students, then let them try using colors in a picture to suggest a mood.

MORE ON COLORS

📖 Paulsen, Gary. The Tortilla Factory. 1995. Harcourt Brace.
   ISBN 0-15-292876-6.

To see the importance of color in a text, take a visually relaxing tour through Gary Paulsen's beautiful book, The Tortilla Factory (illustrated by his wife Ruth Wright Paulsen). In this simple tribute to people who work the land, we see black soil, worked by brown hands ... yellow seeds which grow into green stalks that produce more yellow corn. The whole story is told in a very few words. This is one beginning readers can quickly read on their own. The print is quite large, too. (But you could reprint it to make it

even bigger for young eyes.)

Or ...
try a choral reading, with each student reading just a page or so. The pictures will help those who get stuck on the words. With just two copies of the book, you can easily involve four students. With printouts or copies of just the text, you can involve the whole class.

Think colors!
Organizational structure is often based on change. Think how changing color can play an important role in stories ... changing seasons, or traffic lights, or shadows, or colors in the landscape (as you travel from the mountains to the sea). Ask students to tell a short story involving changes in color. One or two changes are enough for beginners.

BOOKS JUST FOR THE LOVE OF LANGUAGE

Burdett, Lois. <u>A Child's Portrait of Shakespeare</u>. 1995. Black Moss Press. ISBN 0-88753-261-6.

Burdett, Lois. <u>Macbeth for Kids</u>. 1996. Black Moss Press. ISBN 0-88753-279-9.

Burdett, Lois and Coburn, Christine. <u>Twelfth Night for Kids</u>. 1995. Black Moss Press. ISBN 0-88753-233-0.

Do you remember your first introduction to Shakespeare? Were you thrilled? Intrigued? Enchanted? Intimidated? You might find it among the high points of your life were you among Lois Burdett's lucky seven- and eight-year-olds. They enter the world of the bard fearless and full of curiosity, ready to set foot on the stage. How does she do it?

The remarkably talented Lois Burdett, who has taught Shakespeare to second- and third-graders for more than 20 years, inspires her young students with stories and pictures, with retellings of the plays in rhyming couplets (which are reprinted in her books), with costumes (in which her students dress themselves while performing), and with her own obvious love for Shakespeare's world, which shines in all she writes. How do her students, in turn, express their knowledge, understanding, and enthusiasm? Through pictures of characters, diaries, letters from one character to another, historical summaries, and much, much more. You really must see these books to appreciate how much Lois' students know of Shakespeare's world and time. The voice in the students' writings and pictures is remarkable. You will laugh, and you will be amazed. I did and was. I wanted immediately to join Lois' class myself. What a teacher. What a body of work.

Get the books first. Share the rhyming couplets. Then ...

Consider staging a play

If, like Lois, you are fortunate enough to have access to a few stage props (and you can make many yourself) or costumes (they can be simple), you might consider staging one, two, or more scenes. Choreograph one confrontation—perhaps a sword fight. Design a costume on paper or from cloth. Create a model of a stage set. Do a puppet play. Create posters to advertise your production. Or, like Lois and her students, act out several scenes or even a whole play!

Illustrate

Encourage students to draw or color or paint sketches of Shakespeare himself, his children, characters from the plays, London, Stratford on Avon, the Globe theater, or whatever catches their attention. The work of Lois' students will inspire them.

Is this a dagger I see before me? I grope for it but my hand goes throo, Yet it still floats. Now it is bludy not as before and sores like an eagle. Is this an illooshin of my mind? I cannot think strate. My ideas are driving me mad!

Macbeth

Laura Bates, age 7 (writing in character as Macbeth)
from *Lois Burdett*

Macbeth for Kids, 25

Write

Lois' books abound with ideas for diaries, journals, letters, reflections, reviews, etc. You have only to look within. Lois suggests making a map to show where Shakespeare lived or where some of his plays (<u>Hamlet</u>) are located, role playing a newspaper reporter, play reviewer, play goer, or merchant of the time. Write a letter, news column, advertisement, headline story or whatever.

Explore new words

As your young writers enter this language-rich realm, keep track of new words you are learning together. Make lists. Don't let them get away.

Write invitations

If you perform a play (or do short readings or display sketches), you may wish to invite parents or others to enjoy the festivities. This can be part of your writing, too.

Note

Lois' students have performed at the Stratford (Ontario) Festival, the Ontario Legislature, and Southwest Texas State University. Her books are distributed in the U.S. by Firefly Books, Inc., PO Box 1338, Ellicott Station, Buffalo, NY 14205.

Dorros, Arthur. <u>Isla</u>. 1995. Dutton Children's Books. ISBN 0-525-45149-8.

<u>Hay mucho mas que ver</u>. There is much to see, indeed, in this lilting, lively, and colorful tale of exploration. Rosalba and her grandmother travel to <u>la isla</u>, the island where Abuela grew up, and their life is filled with adventures

(a visit to the market, a tour of the rain forest) along the way. Through their experiences, readers have an opportunity to learn some 40 Spanish names and expressions in a text that makes bilingual storytelling seem both easy and inviting.

Bilingual opportunities

If you have bilingual students (or some who'd like to be!), take advantage. Create a bilingual poem, story, list of things to do, thank you note, or whatever! Make a bilingual poster or map. Have fun expanding your language skills.

"Busy" pictures

The illustrations in this text (charmingly rendered by Elisa Kleven) could be called "busy." They're bustling with details and colors. You might wish to talk about this. Do your students see voice in these pictures? (They should!) What's the effect of so much detail? Why does an artist do this? Some of your young artists might wish to experiment with this busy style. Or, they might wish to do a busy picture in a group.

COMBINING TEXT, ARTWORK, & PHOTOS

Ringgold, Faith, Freeman, Linda, and Roucher, Nancy. <u>Talking to Faith Ringgold</u>. 1996. Crown Publishers. ISBN 0-517-88546-8.

Some of the most effective modern literature combines multiple forms of communication. An extraordinary example is Ringgold's combination historical portfolio and personal reflective journal. The layout is spectacular, combining photos of Ringgold and persons who have touched her life, samples of her bewitching art, historical commentary, biography, personal reflections on her work, and—an added bonus!—reflective questions <u>for the reader to think about</u>. If you want to see creative layout and formatting at work, if you want to hear reflective writing at its finest, do not miss this book. It truly is a conversation, one which brings a whole new dimension to the spirit of voice.

Catching the reader's 👁!

Ask students to save (for a month, a quarter, or even a whole year) photos, favorite pictures, bits of artwork or writing, quotations from people who influence them, headlines, book titles, or any bits and pieces that are important, then to create a portfolio collage in the spirit of Ringgold's book. As they add pieces to their pages, ask them to think about colors, placement on the page, making some letters bigger than others. There are no rights and wrongs. It's all about choices, and catching the reader's eye.

BOOKS TO SHOW THE POWER OF INFORMATIONAL WRITING

Today's primary students will be tomorrow's writers of computer manuals, encyclopedia entries, dictionary definitions, greeting cards, copy editors' reference manuals, travel brochures and guidebooks, advertisements, government proposals, cookbooks, personnel and program evaluations, annual reports, and film or theater reviews. An early introduction to the world of informational writing can help make it feel friendly, natural, and within reach. Following are three favorites, all very different in flavor.

Bash, Barbara. <u>Tree of Life</u>. 1989. Sierra Club Books. ISBN 0-316-08322-4.

Did you know the Baobob tree of Africa lives to be 1,000 years old? During its lifetime, it shelters large cats like lions and cheetahs, feeds elephants, and provides shelter and food to dozens of birds and species of insects, monkeys, reptiles, and small mammals. It begins its life as a seedling so small you could easily step on it (though it's tough enough to survive), and winds up (after growing to a height of over 100 feet) crumbling into a ball of light dust, soon swept away by the African wind. Bash's fine and beautifully illustrated book chronicles the remarkable life of this enduring tree. Use the book to teach the concept of life cycles and change over time. Also use it to show that good informational writing often depends as much on illustrations (which could sometimes be charts or graphs) as on text itself.

Doing research

Begin with questions. Let your writers choose their own topics. Encourage them to think up just one or two questions at first! This can be a lot to answer. Then, find the information. Knowing where to look is part of the trick! They should also decide who the audience will be: you the teacher, classmates, parents, or ... ?? Ask them to use the question(s) as a heading or cover, then use pictures and/or text to answer their researchers' questions.

Nussbaum, Hedda, editor. <u>Charlie Brown's Fifth Super Book of Questions and Answers</u>. 1981. Random House. ISBN 0-394-84355-X.

One of the best books ever (all in this series are good) for showing students what good informational writing is all about. The text combines creative and humorous cartoon art with photographs, illustrations, graphs, charts, etc., to answer questions like these:

- What is a machine?
- What makes roller skates roll?
- Is a diving board a machine?
- How does a toaster know when to pop up?
- How does a pencil sharpener work?
- What is an electric shock?
- How did the vacuum cleaner get its name?

The text is clear, easy to understand, and written in a highly engaging manner. It's a good illustration of technical writing: writing that makes specialized information accessible to someone who is not an expert. How do you create good technical writing? You need to become the expert first ....

Becoming experts

Give students a week or so to become the "expert" on some topic of interest: setting up a fish tank, making a taco, potting a plant, binding a book by hand, changing a baby, fixing a toaster (or any simple machine). Then, ask them to do a simple piece of "technical" writing on this topic. They can use photographs, charts, graphs, illustrations, sketches, a series of sketches, labels, dictation, text, audiotape, or any form that gets the message across!

Scieszka, Jon and Smith, Lane. Math Curse. 1995. Viking. ISBN 0-670-86194-4.

Sometimes you just want to have fun with a topic. Especially a topic like math, which is frustrating to many of us! (Yet, fascinating, too!) This whimsical, incredibly creative book explores the way numbers fill our lives, governing everything from time to paychecks. Aaaaaaaagggggghhhh! Is there no escape? Numbers ... can't live with 'em or without 'em. This book makes a fine gift for anyone who has struggled with math as a student or a teacher! And it invites students to recognize that fine writing is sometimes very serious ... but not always!!!!

How it influences me

Take one topic that's always in the news—say, nutrition, music, traffic, movies, fashion and clothing, or weather. Make a collage, sketch a picture or cartoon, write a poem to show how it finds its way into each and every part of our lives, like it or not.

NO MATTER WHICH BOOKS YOU USE

Some activities go with **ALL** books, no matter what the topic or tone. Don't feel you <u>must always</u> follow up with a writing activity. Yuck! Don't forget to read just for the

of it, because you love the language, the story, the characters, or the pictures! At a minimum, you are showing students that you think reading is important, and enjoyable. That is a worthy goal, whether you do anything more or not.

Then, sometimes, you can also ask students to ...

* Write a personal response: How did they like the book?

* Finish the statement "Books are .... "

* Imitate text, illustrations, or format they find impressive

* Take on the role of a character to do a picture, diary entry, or letter

* Draw pictures of what they "see" in their minds as you read

* Predict how a book will end

* Record words they'd like to know more about

* Record new conventions

* Do a choral reading or engage in reader's theater, acting out a text

* Design a poster advertising a favorite book

* Compose a letter to a favorite author, individually, or in a class group

Some Last Thoughts

These few examples should give you some ideas about creative ways to use literature in teaching writing to young writers. Remember ...

1. Students <u>hear</u> voice, fluency, phrasing, detail, and organizational structure long before they can reproduce these things in their own work.

2. As students listen to stories, recipes, informational pieces, journalism, movie reviews, and other pieces you share, they learn to <u>think like readers</u>, to "tune in" to a reader's needs. From this awareness comes the ability to think like a writer, too.

3. <u>Drawing</u> is a valid form of self-expression, too. Picture books, because they are beautifully illustrated, teach children to value their own work as illustrators and artists.

4. <u>Viewing text</u> teaches children about both conventions and layout. They need to see how pictures and text work interactively, and they need to express their own thoughts on this.

5. Children, like all of us, must be <u>critical consumers</u> of what they read and hear. Not all publications are worthy of our reading time. We want them to know the difference. Ask their opinions often. Ask them to think about what they read, or hear. Ask them to anticipate, to pose reader's questions, to have high expectations. If they have high expectations of others, they will have higher expectations of themselves. If they are satisfied with basal readers, they will not ask more from their own writing.

I remember Dick and Jane well. They were always running somewhere or other. Actually, that's all I remember. I never learned about Dick's problems tying his shoe or the grief he felt when Spot got hit by a car. I never heard about the night Jane cried when she found out her grandmother would die or the day she spilled cranberry juice on the rug. Perhaps these events were just too difficult to put into simple English. Let me try.

"See Grandmother die."

"Grieve, Jane, grieve."

"Die, Grandmother, die."

Basal readers have helped millions of children to gain confidence in their reading, but they have also taught those same children that reading could be somewhat, if not totally, boring.

Barry Lane
After the End, 148

---

6. Use the <u>language</u> of writing and reading. Talk to the youngest of your readers/listeners about issues of leads (openings), titles, endings, plot, voice, word choice, fluency, layout, illustrations, fonts, informational writing, narrative writing, story, characters, setting, etc. Make these words part of who they are and how they think.

7. BIG PRINT

often makes it easier for beginners to follow along. You can't rewrite everything, but now and then, rewrite a short text so beginning readers can read with you.

The Reader's Bill of Rights

(from Daniel Pennac, 1994, cited following Pennac's list)

1. The right to not read
2. The right to skip pages
3. The right to not finish
4. The right to reread
5. The right to read anything
6. The right to escapism
7. The right to read anywhere
8. The right to browse
9. The right to read out loud
10. The right to not defend your tastes

The Reader's Bill of Rights is from Daniel Pennac. <u>Better Than Life</u>. 1994. Coach House Press. ISBN 0-889-10-484-0.

Are you a passionate reader? An avid reader? Addicted to books? Or, put it this way: Do you have great difficulty walking past a bookstore? ("I'll just be a minute ... .") Ever been accused of reading too much ("You'll strain your eyes ... .") Got two books going at once? <u>Do</u> you? Three? Four or more? Ha! You're hooked. You owe it to yourself to buy Pennac's delightfully honest and insightful book dedicated to the sheer joy of reading. Reading for the unabashed love of books. Read it to validate the importance of reading aloud to children if we truly want a generation of people who treasure books. It is up to us.

And by the way ...

You can find many, many more picture books reviewed (along with some nifty teaching ideas) in ...

Culham, Ruth. 1998. <u>Picture Books: An Annotated Bibliography with Activities for Teaching Writing</u> (Fifth edition). Portland, OR: Northwest Regional Educational Laboratory.

Chapter 9

WRITING WITH PURPOSE:

MORE THAN STORIES

Writing is thinking.

DON'T LOOK NOW, BUT ...

YOUNG WRITERS CAN WRITE MORE THAN STORIES !!!

> The curriculum guides are wrong. Young children can write nonnarrative and do it well. Let's not deprive them of the chance.
>
> *Sandra Bonin*
>
> "Beyond Storyland" in *Understanding Writing*, 51

Can you teach modes to primary writers?

Absolutely! Ooh, it's the dreaded "m" word, but remember: modes reflect nothing more than different <u>purposes</u> for writing. Even the youngest writers can understand that sometimes you write to express feelings, sometimes to tell a story, sometimes to give someone information, and sometimes to change someone's mind about something.

Here are a few ideas for teaching modes successfully—and by the way, if you hate the very word "modes"—and some people do—use "purposes."

1. Use what's in the environment.

Recipes, for instance, are examples of expository writing. So are the program summaries in <u>TV Guide</u>. Voter pamphlets are part expository, part persuasive. Ads are generally persuasive. Movie and book reviews (including those on the book jackets) are also usually persuasive, with some descriptive thrown in. Menus are descriptive. So are hotel brochures. So are most pamphlets you get at the veterinarian's or dentist's office. Newspaper articles are expository. So are textbooks. Some office memos are, too. Stories and imaginative pieces are everywhere, too; picture books are outstanding sources, but advertising copy can be imaginative, and biographies and journals tell good stories. A restaurant might put a history on the back of a menu; a good zoo or museum often tells its story in literature shared with the public. The point is, various modes, forms, purposes are everywhere. So—look around, collect, and share, just for the sake of building students' awareness about the many different kinds of writing in their environment.

2. Don't feel obligated to "do a unit"

on expository, persuasive, etc. Instead, just find ways to <u>use the language</u> so the terms become familiar to students: e.g., "I went out to eat last week and thought what a great example of <u>descriptive writing</u> was in this menu. Just listen to this <u>description</u> of the colossal fudge dessert ... ."

3. Begin With a Story.

A good story is often a good way into other forms of writing. For instance, a story about a dog might lead to an expository piece on the advantages (or disadvantages) of having a pet. A story about a camping trip could lead to a how-to piece on packing the right stuff for camping outdoors. A descriptive piece on "My Room" could lead to a persuasive essay on why kids should be able to decorate or arrange their own rooms—even if others don't like the results! The secret lies in helping student writers make their own connections by coming up with their own stories, then sharing them and talking about them.

Then, let students <u>who are ready</u> know about their options for writing: e.g., "Ted, you really love cats, I know. This was a great story you wrote about how you found your cat. Let's talk about some other kinds of writing you could do. Remember that <u>description</u> of a snake I read this morning? You could describe your cat, and that could be writing or it could be a picture. I'm also thinking that you know so much about cats, since you own one, that you might want to try some <u>expository</u> writing—that's writing that gives information. An expository paper on cats might tell how to take care of a cat, for instance. What do you think?"

4. Display examples,

both from students and from other sources. You might consider making a **LARGE** poster for each mode of writing you talk about in your school. Then create a wall display. Put the posters up in the hallway or library/media center—somewhere everyone can see. Then attach examples of student writing and outside writing near each poster—stories and story boards near the narrative poster; pictures and descriptive writing near the descriptive poster; brochures, newspaper articles, recipes, lists of directions, how-to writing by students, and other explanatory pieces near the expository poster, and so on. The posters and the examples together will help teach students about different purposes for writing. <u>See the end of this section for samples of text you can use to make **BIG** posters on the purposes for writing.</u>

5. Talk about purposes often.

Use examples from the environment and from your own experience. You might say, "I have been asked to write a paper on how to teach social studies. What kind of writing do you think that paper might be?" Or—"I've just finished a book I think everyone should read. I want to write a paper that tries to convince other people to buy this book. What kind of writing is that?"

6. Don't assess modes—yet.

It's too soon. You don't want to give a "matching quiz" on the five modes of writing, or find out whether primary students are better at expository or descriptive. At this level, the main thing to teach is <u>purpose for writing and the general concept that purpose varies</u> with topic, audience, and author's intent.

Poster-Ready Definitions for Five Modes

On the following pages, you'll see poster-ready definitions for five modes: <u>Narrative, Expository, Persuasive, Descriptive,</u> and <u>Imaginative-Expressive</u>. Use these to make posters. Play with the definitions, changing or expanding them as you wish. Use as many or as few as you like. On each page, you'll also see possible writing tasks/assignments that we hope will give you **IDEAS** for the kinds of writing or topics that might go with each mode.

DESCRIPTIVE

- ♥ **Details**
- ♥ **You can picture it**
- ♥ **See it in your mind**
- ♥ **Hear it, feel it, smell it, taste it**
- ♥ **Seems almost real**

Writing possibilities

- A place I'd like to visit again
- A person I can't get out of my mind
- A corner of my room you'd have to see to believe
- The feeling at the top of the roller coaster (... or ???)
- That first taste (smell) of ...
- Something you might not have looked at close up

EXPOSITORY/ INFORMATIONAL

- ♥ **Gives information**
- ♥ **Tells what, when, where, how**
- ♥ **Explains**
- ♥ **Teaches**

Writing possibilities

- How to make soup (... or ???)
- Directions : How to get from here to ...
- How to care for a dog, cat, rabbit, fish, turtle, or ...
- What makes a good teacher
- How to be a good driver (... or ???)
- How to hit a home run, steal a base (... or ???)
- What the first day of school is like
- What to expect when you visit the dentist

IMAGINATIVE/ EXPRESSIVE

- ♥ Let's pretend
- ♥ It's not real …
- ♥ But it's FUN!!
- ♥ Use your imagination!!
- ♥ What if this happened?
- ♥ Have you ever wondered about?

Writing possibilities

- What if all cars stopped running for a day (… or ???)?
- If you could be part of one television program, what would you choose?
- What would school be like if everyone had computers (… or???)?
- Suppose you could live anywhere in the world you wanted: Would you move? Where would you live?
- School buses are old-fashioned. From now on, we'll get to school by …
- Twenty years from now, some things will be a lot easier. For instance, …
- When I grow up, I will surprise everyone by …
- If I could be a character in a book, I would choose ….
- If I could set up the perfect HOUR (just an HOUR!!) for myself, I would …
- If you could time travel back 100 years, here's what you'd find where our school stands right now ….

232

NARRATIVE

- ♥ Tells a story
- ♥ Tells what happened
- ♥ Plot (solves a problem)
- ♥ Characters
- ♥ Setting : When, where
- ♥ Beginning, details, & end

Writing possibilities:

- A day I'll always want to remember
- A time I surprised myself
- My best (worst) day in school
- An experience with an animal
- A time I had to wait for something
- I made a startling discovery
- I had an adventure with an animal
- I did something I'd like to do over!
- A time I did something I'd been scared to do
- The story of my first cooking adventure, or first ... ???

PERSUASIVE

- ♥ **Tells both sides**
- ♥ **Tells what the writer thinks**
- ♥ **Tells what the writer believes**
- ♥ **Gives good information**
- ♥ **Helps you make up your mind**

Writing possibilities:

- Why shopping is/is not a good way to spend your time
- Why people should/should not have pets
- Why [name a TV show] should/should not be on the air
- Why we should/should not play music in school
- Why kids should/should not be able to roller blade at school
- Why kids should/should not be able to eat snacks in class
- Why people should/should not spend more time getting fit
- Why more kids should/should not play sports

MORE TEACHING IDEAS

An alphabet book
One word or more for each letter, all connected to a central idea, such as animals, hiding places, favorite (or least favorite) foods, things to do in the rain (or snow), things you see at the beach (in the woods, in the city, in a home, on a farm, in a garden, etc.).

"All about ... " books
These might begin with a picture that could have a one word label. Then, the child goes on to write all about ... bees, my dog, my brother, boats, fish, stars, sunshine, birds, school, riding in the car, etc.

A cookbook
Share some favorite but simple recipes with children. Work through one or two as a class—perhaps making the food and sharing it, too! Then, ask children to create their own recipes. You might write one cookbook of serious recipes, and one of inventive recipes no one would really eat. Remember, recipes can be simple; you aren't cooking for a White House luncheon, so it's OK to relax and just have fun. Include Kool-Ade, toast, cereal in a bowl, Jell-O, microwave popcorn, instant hot chocolate—you know—easy but good stuff!

Other how-to books
Kids are experts on how to do all sorts of things: How to shoot marbles, wash the dog (or do other chores), get out of going to the store with mom (or other unappealing activities), get to stay up later than usual, set the table, get your homework done in time to have fun, make your mom (or dad or sibling or friend or someone) feel happy, play Nintendo, bat a ball, shop, keep from getting bored in the car, plant a garden, get rid of mosquitoes, stop the hiccups, etc. Start with a list of things various people in the class are good at. There's nothing like hearing other ideas to help you get ideas of your own. Then create a book of how-to ideas—perhaps to share or trade with another class.

Newspaper articles

Newspapers are simply accounts of what's happening right now. Why not let students draft their own "what's happening" stories? They can report on doings at school, in their own classroom, during lunch, after school activities, sports, neighborhood news, or family events of general interest.

Why you should

Young children are masterful crafters of arguments to persuade adults that they should see the world differently. Capitalize on this talent by letting them put some of their ideas in writing: e.g., why someone should (or shouldn't) ... read a certain book, watch a film or TV show, buy a given product, eat a certain food, make new friends, complain if something goes wrong, drive at the speed limit, own a pet, let their feelings show, etc. What do your young writers feel strongly about?

Other forms to try

Lists, poems, jokes, riddle books, menus, posters, rules (like rules for the swimming pool), greeting cards, buttons, stickers, labels for products to be sold, advertisements. Borrow from the writing all around us, always, <u>always</u> talking about how different writing serves different purposes.

JUST A MOMENT ...
NOT A WRITING EVENT

Writing does not always have to be a **BIG DEAL**. Some of the most useful writing occurs when we just take time out, a moment or two, to use writing to think, to pose a question, to record a thought, or to make a suggestion. Following are a few ideas for weaving writing naturally into the fabric of your everyday classroom life without feeling the need to commit an *ACT OF WRITING*.

- A question I'd like answered today is ...
- Something I hope to learn today
- One important thing I learned today (this week)
- Thank you notes to anybody
- One question I'd like to ask the author of a book we just read (you can share these aloud, with students' permission)
- One mark of punctuation I'd like to know more about
- Something I'm curious about
- Something I noticed that was different today
- Something I wish our class could do is ...
- A word I wish I could spell is ...
- My list of rules for the class/lunchroom/playground
- Three reasons to read this book/see this film/watch this TV show (or not!)
- One thing I remember is ... [after lesson in math, social studies, geography, art]
- I predict ... [what I think this lesson will be about]
- Journal of change [plants, pets, landscape, visiting baby!!]

Chapter 10

THE JOY

OF PORTFOLIOS

Are your students creating portfolios? If not, are you exploring the possibilities? The advantages are many. Portfolios offer students

📁 An opportunity to <u>save pieces of work</u> that might otherwise be lost in the shuffle

📁 A way of <u>visually capturing change</u>, growth, & acquisition of new skills

📁 A chance to <u>reflect</u> on the hows & so whats of creating, thinking, & learning

📁 An opportunity to take <u>a close-up look at the process</u> of learning, not just the tangible products

📁 A chance to be <u>managers of their own learning</u>, by keeping track of growth & setting goals for future work

A student portfolio is a thoughtfully selected sampling of work that traces that student's learning, growth, and reflective thoughts over a period of time. It's part scrapbook, part learning log, part intellectual journey. The best portfolios (if there is any such thing) seem to be those in which the creator invests enough of him- or herself that browsing through the portfolio is like sitting down for a conversation with the student him- or herself.

A "telling" portfolio might have some of these characteristics:

📁 It would be <u>highly individual</u>, reflective of the student. It would not look like everyone else's portfolio.

📁 It <u>wouldn't be too big</u>. You'd be able to see that the student had not just tossed everything in, but had thoughtfully, reflectively chosen just those pieces that would show something important.

📁 <u>You could "read" it</u>, almost like a book. The portfolio might say, "Look how confident I am!" Or it might say, "Look how many writing or reading skills I've gained this year." It might even say, "This was a year I'll always remember!"

📁 It would contain some <u>reflection</u>, either recorded or written. Perhaps a picture. Looking through it, you would get a sense of the student looking within her own work, saying, "This is what I do well. Be sure to notice this. I feel good about this skill .... I'm going to work on this."

One Student's Sample

On the following pages, you'll see samples from one student's portfolio. Sara Knight was in grade two when she created this portfolio to show her growth in writing and reading skills. In addition to the work shown here, Sara included in her portfolio a favorite book, <u>Rotten Ralph</u>, that she read to her mom (with great feeling and inflection) at the end of her second-grade year, during their student-parent-teacher conference. Sara had spent much of grade one as a nonreader and beginning reader. For both Sara and her mother, this independent reading was a moment of exuberant celebration and personal victory. "You did it, you did it," was the message in mom's tear-filled eyes and on Sara's smiling face. Such is the power of the portfolio. <u>Sara, thank you so much for sharing your work.</u>

One time I got really Scared. I was in the kitchen eating dinner. My little sister came in the kitchen and she touched the burner. My mom took her finger and ran it under water. We got really scared it looked all black and blue. My mom put a bandaide on it.

Name Sara
Daily Reading File

Date May 22
Sara
DAILY SCORE
Summary
Opinion/
Support

Name Sara
S.O.S.
Amelia Badelia
Pages Read 5-A8
Duck

December 1, 1994

Dear
Mr. Clinton How Do You like living there? I'm learing abot Washingson D.C. I'm 7 Years Olda and My Nameis Sara Knight. I Knewthe Flag has 50 Stars in it. They Stand for the united States.

The rain forest is very hot. Almost all the animals live in the rain forest. There are 3 layers in the rain forest. The canopy and under story and the forest floor. The canopy and half the animals animals in it. If You lived in the rain forest You would be used to the weather but You mom do anymore But You can do stuff like the rain frest p shot buying bananas a coffee

She was born in Heroshima Japan. She was very happy she Saw some sad luck things like a fire and the Sun. She liked to run She liked the Sun. When she was 12 When she died there is a memona in her ohnr.

9 + 1 9 9 4
DAILY SCORE
Summary
Support
+ 3 - 13
house
ant and his
row will not

240

THE WORKS OF
SARA KNIGHT

Fall Samples of Writing...

Sara Knight
What I'm Thankful For...

My mom and Dad and MY Sitre to Be caZ thaY haep me when I'mSick

Personal essay

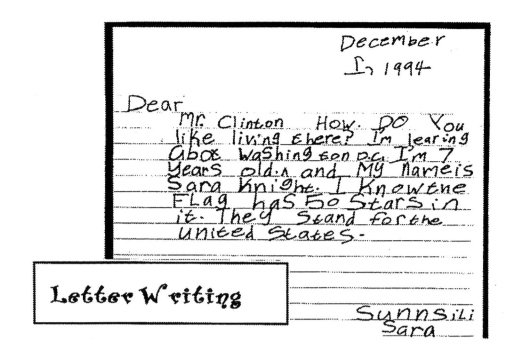

December I, 1994

Dear
Mr. Clinton How DO You like living there? I'm learing abot Washington D.C. I'm 7 Years old. and My Nameis Sara Knight. I Knowthe Flag has 50 Stars in it. They stand forthe united States.

Sunnsili
Sara

Letter Writing

Mid-Year Samples

One time I got really scared. I was in the kitchen eating dinner. My little sister came in the kitchen and she touched the burner. My mom took her finger and ran it under water. we got really scared it looked all black and blue. mom put a bandaide on it.

Personal Narrative

242

Reflection on . . .

Sadako and the Thousand Paper Cranes. Eleanor Coerr. 1977.
ISBN 0-440-47465-5.

She was born in Heroshima
Japan. She was very happy she
Saw some good luck signs like
a sider and the sun. She liked
to run She liked she
died She was 12 When she
there is a memoria in
her ohnr.

ANTEATER

I'm going to tell about how the anteaters eats. an anteeaters eats trmites
Its too hard to eat anithng else cause they dont have teeth. The anteater has
no teeth So The anteeote Suck food up With his long stick
a Bug crawling on The Ground he'll Scoop it up with his big tongue. If there is
anteater has large claws and a big nose. They are noe very big The
anteater has fun!

Expository/Research Writing

243

Reading Reflections
Beginning & End of Year

Name Sara

S.O.S.
Title TheCARROt SEED   Date 9-19994
Author Krauss

DAILY SCORE
Summary ____
Opinion/ ____
Support

Summary
it   was   adat   a boy howe
Planted a CARR SEED and
his mom And DaD and his
Big brother said tt
Drow an   it   grow Will not

Pages Read 3-13

Name Sara

Daily Reading File

DAILY SCORE
Summary ____
Opinion/ ____
Support

Name Sara   Date May 27

S.O.S.
Title Come Back ameLia BedeLia   Pages Read 5-A8
Author Lynn   Sweat

Summary
ameLla Bedella trid A Buck
of jobs But thay did't wrak

244

Spring Samples

The rain forest is very hot. Almost all the animals live in the rain forest. There are 5 layers in the rain forest. There are the under story and the emergent and forest floor there are almost half the World animals in it. If You lived in the rain forest you would be used to the weather but not many do anymore But You can help the rain frest BY not buying stuff like bananas a coffee

On Thursday We Went to the zoo. there Was a LOOG line It lock a While to get there When We got inside We ate lunck I Sat on the statue of a gorilla head. He didn't mind I learned

that a lot of the animals that live in the zoo are endangered. My favorite part Was runing!

My Trp to The ZOO

Sara   Jane

REFLECTIONS (DICTATED)

Favorite literary character ...

This is Rotten Ralph. I like cats and that is one reason I chose him as my favorite character. I own a cat that reminds me of Ralph. One time he pulled off a tale cloth while we were still eating. Rotten Ralph belongs to a girl with the same name as me.

On myself and my life ...

My name is Sara Knight. I go to Beaver Acres School. I love sports, mostly soccer. In my spare time I look in a book. If it is about a castle, I draw a castle. This year I have learned a lot about Japan. I have improved the most in reading.

On school ...

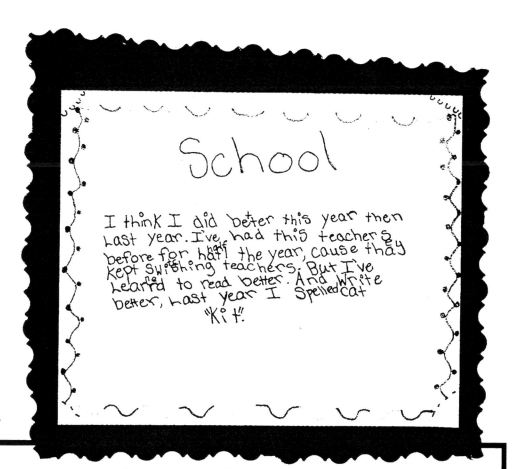

School

I think I did better this year then Last year. I've had this teachers before for half the year, cause thay kept switching teachers. But I've learnd to read better. And write better, Last year I Spelled cat "Kit".

On writing ...

Me as a Writer!

I think I am a good writer. I like writing about my family and me. Sometimes I look out my window. There is a tree I like to climb. I like to write about it. Mostly I get ideas from books. I write something similar to what I read. I've written a book called My Grandma is a Ghost. I got the idea from watching "Casper" at my grandma's house. When I grow up I want to be a writer.

Sara Knight!!!!!!

WHAT WE LEARN FROM SARA'S PORTFOLIO

Even a quick glance at Sara's portfolio shows her to be a young writer with a growing sense of self and voice. She has a good eye and ear for detail: "Anteeters eats trmites. It's too hard to eat anithng else cause they dont have teeth" (from **Anteater,** expository piece).

Through the year, her sentence fluency and word choice grow by leaps and bounds (compare her fall personal essay to the spring informational writing on the rain forest). She is beginning to use words like "endangered," "emergent," and "similar" with ease.

In Sara's self-reflections, we hear bursts of confidence: "I think I am a good writer," and a real sense of herself: "In my spare time I look in a book"—the source, she tells us, of many writing ideas! We see her conventional control grow, too, as she begins to use capitals, commas, and periods with confidence, to include more apostrophes, and to tackle the spelling of even difficult words with expanding skill.

Notice too how many different kinds of writing Sara attempts through the year: e.g., literary response, personal narrative, informational writing, letter writing. With such diverse experience, we can expect her skills to grow quickly. We also discover that she has a strong link to her family (this shows in her sketches, photographs, and writing), and that she loves books.

Thanks again, Sara, for sharing so much of yourself and your work.

A Plan For Using Portfolios In Your Classroom

Would you like to make portfolios part of your classroom experience? Here's a quick plan intended to help you simplify the process and make it all manageable.

Step 1: Save

At the beginning of the year (or whenever you start), just be pack rats for a while and collect stuff. Horde. Encourage students to keep a working file of art or writing they consider special. They might want to draw pictures or write down names to represent favorite books, too. These are fun to remember!

Step 2: Talk

Talk about what a portfolio is: part scrapbook, part special collection of favorite work or work students are proud of. You might use a photo album to help students see how pictures record change over time. A good portfolio records changes, too, only they are changes in your work, not changes in how you look.

Talk about the kinds of things that could go into a portfolio: pictures, sketches, photographs; first writing with real letters or real words or a whole sentence; first book; first writing that shows punctuation; a list of new words; a dictated story; or anything that is specially important to a student! They should use their imaginations! Stress the importance of not putting EVERYTHING into the portfolio. Yes, it's tempting! But, boy, it will get huge. And then it will be hard for someone else to read and appreciate. You might use Sara's portfolio as an example. Notice how Sara carefully selected a FEW important things. Yet, how much we learn about her!

Step 3: Share

Share books in which writers/artists talk reflectively about their own work. This helps students see why we save work, and what it shows about us. Two good choices are

1. Ringgold, Faith and Freeman, Linda. <u>Talking to Faith Ringgold</u>. 1996. Crown Publishers. ISBN 0-517-88546-8.

2. Littlechild, George. <u>This Land Is My Land</u>. 1993. Children's Book Press. ISBN 0-89239-119-7.

Step 4: Get Some BIG Containers

They do not have to be fancy. You can use paper bags (though they do wear out), or even cloth or mesh bags. Students can stitch their own! Another easy-to-put-together container is made from two matching pieces of tag board of the sort often given away to inquiring teachers by frame shops (who have extra odd sizes). Remember, not all portfolios in your class have to be the same size. Use cloth or paper strips (folded the short way into the letter "W") to create an accordion effect so you can open the container WIDE. Keep these portfolios in a cut-off refrigerator box in one corner—or, do as Sara's teacher did, and ask students to keep them right by their desks. Handy for putting things in!

Step 5: Get Festive!!

Encourage students to decorate their portfolios in any way that makes them seem special, using stickers, sketches, self-portraits, words, magazine cut-outs, etc. Some teachers ask students to add words or pictures to the covers to hint at what's inside.

Step 6: Make Choices

Every two, three, or four weeks, ask students to go through their collections of "stuff," and to choose a piece to go into the portfolio. Think of it like "shopping" and making a choice. You can't put in everything! Be selective.

Choose a piece that shows something special: something the student just learned, something new the student tried.

Step 7: Reflect

Ask students to include reflections on themselves, their work, pieces they have chosen, favorite books, the class itself, new skills, etc. You will need to help by reading reflections from people like Faith Ringgold and George Littlechild, or by keeping your own portfolio and reading reflections on your own work. An easy way to begin is to ask students to compare two or more pieces of work created at different times (perhaps three or four weeks apart). What differences do they see? How has their work changed? Reflections can be written or dictated. If you're lucky enough to have a parent or older student who will help with this, by all means take advantage! Reflections do not need to be miles long to be good.

High on our new list is teaching children how to read their own work. We teach them how to read books but not how to read their own writing. I see too many folders and portfolios filled with papers that reveal little significant change. Unless we show children how to read their writing, their work will not improve.

Donald Graves
A Fresh Look At Writing, xvi

Step 8: Keep Your Own Portfolio

Do it! You'll be amazed what you will learn about yourself. Start with something fairly simple: "My Year." You could write a reflection predicting what the year will be like. Include some poetry, letters, other short writings, artwork, or photographs. Now and then reflect on a favorite book, something you've learned from teaching, something a student taught you, a favorite moment, something you'd do differently, the joy (or agony!) of a field trip, a personal goal, a person (or film, play, etc.) that influenced you, or—anything at all! Your students will love having you share with them your selections and self-reflections. You and they will come to know you in a whole new way! And you'll have your portfolio stories to share forever more.

More ideas

On the following pages, you'll find many more ideas for putting portfolios to work in your classroom, including

A proposed <u>schedule</u> for a portfolio-based parent conference
First graders' <u>criteria</u> for good stories & good writing (they <u>can</u> make good choices!)
Ideas for <u>self-reflection</u>
A sample <u>parent letter</u>
<u>Suggestions</u> for what could go into a portfolio (you should not follow our suggestions too literally)

These are only ideas, after all. Your classroom is unique, so you and your students should create portfolios that capture that special instructional flavor that is yours alone. Have fun!!

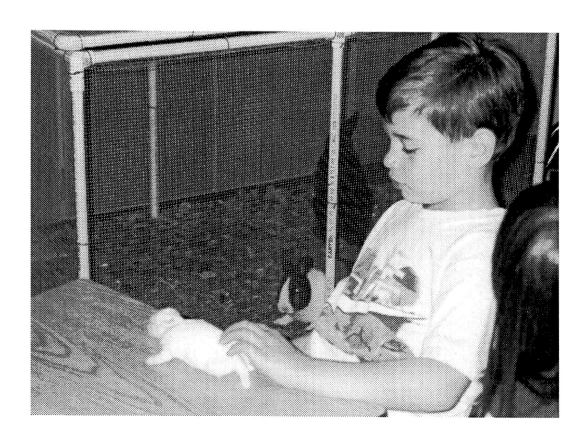

STUDENT-LED PORTFOLIO CONFERENCE: A PARENT-STUDENT CONVERSATION

1. **INVITATION**
   Make and take home an invitation that gives your parents the date and time of the conference.

2. **INTRODUCTION**
   Practice and take responsibility for introducing your parents to your teachers and other visitors in the class.

3. **WORKING FOLDER**
   Show all the things you have collected in your folder.

4. **PORTFOLIOS**
   Show things you have selected for your portfolio and explain why you made these choices.

5. **REFLECTION**
   Share **ONE** self-reflection that tells
   ♥ Your main strengths
   ♥ Your goals
   ♥ What you want to work on

6. **CLOSING:**
   Ask parents to write to you and show them where they can make a comment to the teacher or ask for another appointment.

GOOD LUCK!
You can be proud of the work you have done this term. You wil do fine!

THINGS THAT COULD GO IN YOUR PORTFOLIO

ARITHMETIC
- ♥ Story problems
- ♥ Workbook
- ♥ Favorite number facts
- ♥ Math outside of class
- ♥ Things I know and want to learn

READING
- ♥ Key words (choose 10)
- ♥ Reader (pick one story)
- ♥ Fairy tale booklet
- ♥ Oral reading
- ♥ Favorite story read to me
- ♥ Funny things I've learned about reading

LANGUAGE ARTS
- ♥ Literary response journal
- ♥ Book reports
- ♥ Printing book
- ♥ Creative writing
- ♥ Writer's notebook

ART
- ♥ Favorite picture
- ♥ Family picture
- ♥ Copy of illustration
- ♥ Picture of a painting I like
- ♥ All the different art mediums I know (cut/paste, paint, crayon, pencil, etc.)
- ♥ Favorite artwork of mine

SCIENCE
♥ Science project
♥ Experiment
♥ Observation
♥ Film
♥ Articles
♥ Notes
♥ Diagrams

SOCIAL STUDIES
♥ Project
♥ Bulletin board
♥ Poster
♥ Oral report
♥ Newspaper headlines
♥ Verbal retellings of news reports
♥ Interesting historical facts

OTHER
♥ All about me
♥ Individual report card
♥ What I've learned
♥ What I like/dislike
♥ Something new
♥ Something I'm proud of
♥ Bet you didn't know

LETTING PARENTS KNOW ABOUT PORTFOLIOS

It's a good idea to let parents share in the portfolio process. If a child has a "works in progress" folder or "working file," that work can go home for parents to review. Portfolios can go home too, of course—but sometimes they do not return! Notice how the third-grade teacher whose letter to parents is reprinted on the following page solves this problem nicely by inviting parents to review the bulk of their children's work, and also making them welcome to visit the school to view the much smaller portfolios if they wish to do so. Ms. Tucker's letter also informs parents about the purposes of the portfolio and the school's plans for dealing with it at the end of the year. Notice how parents are also encouraged to reflect with their child on her work for the year, not just to read it or do a critique, but to actually identify areas of new growth and strength.

DEAR PARENT —

This year your child has worked on putting together a portfolio of her writing. A portfolio is an individual, purposeful collection of student work that helps each student see personal effort, progress, and achievement. Both student and teacher worked on selecting the contents of the writing portfolio. It also contains student self-reflection—your child writing about her work and her goals as a writer. The purposes of the writing portfolio are

- ♣ To focus on what the student CAN do, and on how her writing has improved over time;
- ♣ To provide a written, documented record of your child's writing progress; and
- ♣ To give the student an opportunity and a place to record her thinking about what she has learned.

Today, your child is bringing home a writing folder (different from the portfolio), that contains the majority of this year's writing efforts. From this folder, your young writer and I have each selected favorite works. *These will be saved here at school in the child's writing portfolio.* Included in the portfolio is a statement about why we chose the works we did. The portfolio will be passed along to next year's teacher for your child to use in that classroom. We expect your child's personal writing portfolio to be part of her instruction for years to come.

I hope you will enjoy looking at your child's writing folder and seeing the progress that I see. Please talk with your child about her writing. Ask questions that help you both reflect on what was learned. Feel free to call me or stop by If you would like to see the writing portfolio itself.

Sincerely,

Cissy Tucker
Grade three instructor
Scarselli Elementary

PORTFOLIO BAG

An idea for introducing the portfolio concept to your students

Prepare a personal portfolio bag containing three to five items that show who you are. Decorate the bag to show even more about you. Your items might include pictures, books, sports equipment, toys, clothing, awards, special foods, or <u>anything else</u> that tells something about who you are. Put your name on the bag. Then, plan to tell everyone about the bag, how you decorated it, and what you put in it. These portfolios will help us all get to know each other better.

Maggie Fridman

<u>Redefining the Boundaries of Portfolio Assessment,</u>
Ohio Council of Teachers of English, Vol. 35, No. 1, Spring/Summer 1994, p. 55

Once your students have gone through this step, you can easily show them how their writing and other work also tells important things about who they are!

258

Leading psychologists and educators in a number of fields—including math, science, social studies, and, to some degree, reading—agree that it is particularly important for children to learn how to learn. The knowledge explosion makes it virtually impossible for people to keep up with any given field. Instead of cramming children with facts they may not need, the schools must help children learn to learn, to find the information they need and apply it.

Donald Graves and Virginia Stuart, 1985, p. 84

SOURCES CITED

Bonin, S. (1988). Beyond storyland: Young writers can tell it other ways. In T. Newkirk & N. Atwell (Eds.), *Understanding Writing*. Portsmouth, NH: Heinemann.

Bridge, S. (1988). Squeezing from the middle of the tube. In T. Newkirk & N. Atwell (Eds.), *Understanding Writing*. Portsmouth, NH: Heinemann.

Calkins, L.M. (1994). *The art of teaching writing* (rev. ed.). Portsmouth, NH: Heinemann.

Chew, C. (1985). Instruction can link writing and reading. In J. Hansen, T. Newkirk, & D. Graves (Eds.), *Breaking ground: Teachers relate reading and writing in the elementary school*. Portsmouth, NH: Heinemann.

Chiseri-Strater, E. (1988). Reading to Mr. Bear. In T. Newkirk & N. Atwell (Eds.), *Understanding writing*. Portsmouth, NH: Heinemann.

Clay, M. (1979). *What did I write?* Portsmouth, NH: Heinemann.

Fein, S. (1993). *First drawings: Genesis of visual thinking*. Pleasant Hill, CA: Exelrod Press.

Fox, M. (1993). *Radical reflections*. New York, NY: Harcourt Brace.

Fraser, J., & Skolnick, D. (1994). *On their way: Celebrating second graders as they read and write*. Portsmouth, NH: Heinemann.

Graves, D.H. (1994). *A fresh look at writing*. Portsmouth, NH: Heinemann.

Graves, D.H., & Stuart, V. (1985). *Write from the start*. New York, NY: Signet.

Hilliker, J. (1985). Labeling to beginning narrative: Four kindergarten children learn to write. In T. Newkirk & N. Atwell (Eds.), *Understanding writing*. Portsmouth, NH: Heinemann.

Mathews, K. (1985). A child composes. In T. Newkirk & N. Atwell (Eds.), *Understanding writing*. Portsmouth, NH: Heinemann.

Murray, D. (1985). *A writer teaches writing* (2nd ed.). Boston, MA: Houghton Mifflin.

Newkirk, T. (1989). *More than stories: The range of children's writing*. Portsmouth, NH: Heinemann.

Newman, J. (1984). *The craft of children's writing*. Portsmouth, NH: Heinemann.

Paulsen, G. (1993). *Dogteam*. New York, NY: Delacorte Press.

Pennac, D. (1994). *Better than life*. Toronto, Canada: Coach House Press.

Rynkofs, J.T. (1985). *Sending your writing folders home*. In T. Newkirk & N. Atwell (Eds.), *Understanding writing*. Portsmouth, NH: Heinemann.

Sowers, S. (1985). *Six questions teachers ask about invented spelling*. T. Newkirk & N. Atwell (Eds.), *Understanding writing*. Portsmouth, NH: Heinemann.

Steig, W. (1977). *Amos and Boris*. New York, NY: Puffin Books.

ALSO RECOMMENDED

Culham, R., (1998, 5th edition). *Picture books: An annotated bibliography with activities for teaching writing for teaching writing*. Portland, OR: Northwest Regional Educational Laboratory.

Dozens of outstanding picture books for all ages (primary through adult) are reviewed and thoroughly annotated. Listings are alphabetical by trait (books to teach ideas, books to teach organization, books to teach voice, etc.). The new edition also includes many excellent teaching ideas that integrate reading and writing.

Spandel, V., & Culham, R. (1995). *Writing from the inside out*. Portland, OR: Northwest Regional Educational Laboratory. [Distributed through IOX, 5301 Beethoven Street, Suite 109, Los Angeles, CA 90066-7061. Order by phone: (310) 822-3275.]

This book features numerous teaching ideas for students who are experienced, fluent writers capable of creating two-paragraph, multisentence texts, and ready for development of revision skills. Lessons are based on the six-trait model, and encourage reading aloud, teaching students to assess, providing opportunities for students to revise the work of others, and sharing your own writing in order to teach revision.

Spandel, V., & Stiggins, R.J. (1997). *Creating writers*. New York, NY: Longman. [Order by phone: 1-800-822-6339.]

This text includes an introduction to high-quality classroom assessment and thoughts on 21st-century writing, a newly updated six-trait scoring guide with many practice samples of student writing that cross multiple forms and grade levels (suggested teacher scores included), an indepth look at the writing process, ideas for adapting the six-trait model to expository and research writing, a Spanish translation of the student scoring guide, ideas for teaching revision, grading students, and managing response groups successfully, and tips on bringing parents on board to support new assessment strategies.